D1413244

The Book of US

A guide to scrapbooking about relationships

reflections

2

The Story of
Grandma & Me

us

by Angie Pedersen

Dedication. To David, James and Joanne—my most *favoritest* relationships of all

Acknowledgements. Heartfelt thanks to Sara Naumann for the beautiful foreword; to my creative team at One Scrappy Site for their support, especially Jill, Wanda, Rhonda, Holle and Nancy for their help with feedback and projects; to my parents and in-laws for making sure my kids got to enjoy their summer; to Andrea Steed of ScrapJazz.com and Jen Newton of ScrapsAhoy.com for providing such excellent resources to the scrapbooking world; to David Kellin for the continued use of his prompts; to Sarah Plinsky for encouraging me in the darkness; to all my project contributors for sharing your talent; and finally, Elaine Floyd —everyone should have such a champion.

The Book of Us. ©2005, Angie Pedersen. All rights reserved. This book may not be duplicated in any form without written permission from the publisher, except in the form of brief excerpts or quotations for the purposes of review.

First Edition. Printed and bound in the USA

09 08 07 06 05   5 4 3 2 1

Library of Congress Control Number: 2004117129

ISBN: 1-930500-17-3

Limit of Liability & Disclaimer. The author and publisher have used their best efforts in preparing this book. The author and publisher make no warranty of any kind, expressed or implied, with regard to the instructions and suggestions contained in this book. The scrapbook page layouts throughout this book are used with permission.

Published by:
EFG, Inc.; (314) 762-9762

Distributed to the trade by:
North Light Books
an imprint of F&W Publications, Inc.
4700 East Galbraith Road
Cincinnati, OH 45236
fax: (513) 531-4082
tel: (800) 289-0963

Foreword

Life, I've come to realize, is all about celebrating what you love.

For most of us, that's about relationships. It's how my best friend can still make me laugh the same way she did back in second grade. It's the way my husband's smile somehow makes even the worst problem just a little less critical. And it's how my mother still reminds me to bring a sweater when it's cold outside.

It's not about me. It's not about them. Instead, it's about us.

Creating a scrapbook is simply a way to turn your husband's smile, your girlfriend's giggles, your mother's reminders and all those other relationships into memories. And guess what? You don't need an expensive camera. You don't have to be a fabulous writer. All it requires, really, is a relationship. An "us".

Take a minute now to think of one person in your life who deserves to be celebrated, one person you admire, spend time with, laugh with and talk to. Who is it?

I consider myself lucky to know a fabulous woman of strength, integrity and creativity. From her I've learned so many lessons, both personal and professional. She's the woman who built a 25-year-old business, Hot Off The Press, from a single book self-published on her kitchen table. She's taken everything life has to offer, handling both the good and not-so-good with grace and style. If you know Hot Off The Press, then you know Paulette Jarvey.

It's because of Paulette that I first started scrapbooking eight years ago. Of course, scrapbooking has changed a lot since then. Nowadays, it's not about having an album filled with all the latest tools and supplies. It's about the who, not the how. And those changes are actually why I created the first sarabook™—made, coincidentally, for Paulette!

You see, it was a way to celebrate my relationship with her—the "us" that made up such a good team. The result? A handmade book, totally customized to reflect her personality—which in Paulette's case means a book made with one-of-a-kind purple handmade papers and filled with quotes and sayings about art and creativity. And the book was simply bound with fibers, because I know Paulette can't resist gorgeous fuzzy fibers.

The book took me about a month to make, since I hand-stamped and textured each page, then researched quotes and sayings and typed them on my computer. I shopped. I typed. I stamped until my hands ached. Was it worth it? Absolutely. Not only did I have a blast creating this book, but Paulette loved it. (Yes, she cried when she got it.) And after that, came the sarabooks™ product line of papers, quotes, fibers and blank books based on the book.

Ironically, the most rewarding thing about this little handmade gift book is still, well…it's still that original little handmade gift book. It's not really about having a product line with your name on it. It's not teaching classes all over the world. And although it's quite a thrill to see someone else's sarabook™ on the front cover of a book like this one, what it really comes down to is celebrating the "us". And that goes back to the one thing I know for sure:

Life is all about celebrating what you love. So grab your papers, your scissors and your glue—and think for just a minute about that person you'd like to celebrate. Then go scrapbook it. You'll be glad you did.

Sara Naumann
Hot Off the Press
www.hotp.com

[*Angie's note:* See sarabook™ examples on pages 1, 33, 37, 56, 57, 66, 67 and 103.]

Contents

Welcome
pages 4 to 7

Our history
pages 8 to 23

Our themes
pages 24-39

Our perspectives
pages 40 to 53

Our celebrations
pages 54 to 65

Our love
pages 66 to 79

Our family
pages 80 to 95

Our group
pages 96 to 109

Our friendship
pages 110 to 123

Circle journals
pages 124 to 139

My gift to you
pages 140 to 151

Index & Dessert
pages 152 to 160

*(Library cards and pockets created by Jennifer Wellborn.
See album on pages 126 and 127.)*

25 MEMORIES
OF 25 YEARS

CELEBRATING THE FRIENDSHIP OF
DAVID PEDERSEN AND MATTHEW PILCHARD
1977-2002 (AND BEYOND)

WEDDING

SEPTEMBER 6TH, 1977
THE FIRST DAY OF SCHOOL

Welcome!

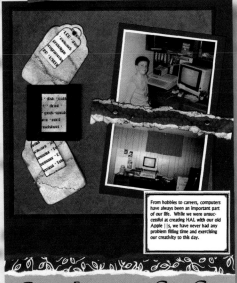

GEEKS FROM THE GET-GO

From hobbies to careers, computers have always been an important part of our life. While we were unsuccessful at creating HAL with our old Apple ||s, we have never had any problem filling time and exercising our creativity to this day.

My husband David recently celebrated the 25th anniversary of meeting his best friend. Part of this milestone was creating a scrapbook of 25 memories... We made a Book of Us.

SUPPLIES: Paper is Paper Adventures, Lasting Impressions and Chatterbox. Cardstock is Pebbles in My Pocket and Bazzill Basics. Fonts are Aphasia, LCD and Albertus Medium. Buttons are Junkitz. Inks are Ranger. Brads and silver coil are Boxer Scrapbooks.

25 Memories of 25 Years
by Angie Pedersen with David Pedersen

These layouts are from the Friendship-Anniversary album I made for my husband and his best friend. David chose the photos, memorabilia, titles and journaling. I created the basic album design and layouts. It was really rewarding to work on this project with him—I got to see his creative side and learned a lot about his friendship with Matt! The friendship that Matt and David have shared is unique in it's longevity and strength.

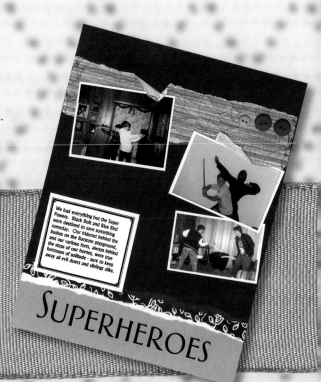

We had everything but the Super Powers. Black Bolt and Blue Bird were destined to save something someday. Our hideout behind the bushes on the Barstow playground, and our various forts, always behind the steps of our homes, were true fortresses of solitude - sure to keep away all evil doers and siblings alike.

SUPERHEROES

When books are opened you discover you have wings.

—Helen Hayes

Books tap the wisdom of our species—the greatest minds, the best teachers—from all over the world and from all our history. And they're patient.

—Carl Sagan

The instruction we find in books is like fire. We fetch if from our neighbors, kindle it at home, communicate it to others, and it becomes the property of all.

—Voltaire

*I*n putting together David's album, I couldn't help but notice the strength of his relationship with Matt—all of their shared experiences, all of the jokes, all the things they talked about and lived through together.

It forced me to think about the relationships in my own life and how rich my life is because of them. That realization made the time I spent with these people all the more precious and worth preserving.

A scrapbook is the perfect place to celebrate relationships. This book gives you examples of scrapbooks that tell what people appreciate and value about their relationships and how they affect their lives.

The layouts I chose for *The Book of Us* describe the *relationship* between the subjects—more so than just a picture of two or more people and a few eloquent words.

Why make a "Book of Us"?

Although relationships figure prominently in most scrapbooks—layouts feature siblings, spouses, friends and co-workers—what's missing is journaling about the meaning behind those relationships.

In creating a book about her children, a mother can journal her feelings about why it's important to her to be their mother, what she values about the time she spends with her children and why her children love having her for a mom. In creating layouts about her children and their friends, she can write down specific examples of the interactions between the friends and what they add to each others' lives.

Relationships are about intimacy and connections with other people. Relationships are two-way, cause and effect, providing support and balance. By taking the time to document relationships in a scrapbook,

The Book of Quotations

Collected By

Matthew N. Pilchard

&

David J. Pedersen

QUOTES

Pointing a gun at a police officer, can we waste him for this?
I think so.
Yeah.
You know this kind of thing starts in the home.
It's the educational system.
No, the new Math drives 'em nuts.
Right to the streets.
Really?
Yeah.

Gregory Hines and Billy Crystal
Running Scared

You know, I did a little clothes shopping over here at the K-Mart. I think when I say K-Mart we are all hip to the fact that I mean style central. Picked up a couple of short sleeve suits and a Century 21 blazer for the holidays.

—Dennis Miller

you honor how each relationship has enhanced and blessed your life.

My goal with this book is to illustrate the different ways you can create a "Book of Us". Within these pages I've compiled many ideas for different angles you can take in approaching your own project. I encourage you to create an album that completes the statement, "This is a Book of US because it shows how we...." (met, enjoy spending time together, support each other...).

In defining the core of your relationships, you remind yourself of your priorities and the goodness in your life. Because your life is linked with others, you also have the opportunity to recognize the goodness you contribute to their lives.

"Us" as opposed to "Me"

As you approach your Book of Us, note that many layout topics are similar to topics offered in my first book, *The Book of Me*. Here's the distinction. In a Book of Me layout, you might journal about why your role as mother is important to you. The same topic in a Book of Us layout would focus on the two-way relationship. A Book of Us layout about motherhood would describe both ends of that relationship, both mother and child, and where they meet in the middle.

Here are some basic ideas for you to explore:

❑ What things define your relationship?

❑ What illustrates the key features of the activities you do together and how you relate to each other?

❑ What are the things that each of you brings to the relationship?

❑ What are the strengths and weaknesses of each person that balance the relationship?

❑ What do you depend on (skills, talents, strengths, etc) in the other person or people?

❑ Write about why it's important to you to be in this relationship.

❑ Ask the other person or people what your relationship means to them and include their words.

The Book of US is different from other layout idea books because it encourages you to dig deeper into your journaling to express the essential aspects of your relationships. The album ideas encourage you to recognize the interconnectedness of your scrapbooking subjects and to honor these people.

Share the stories of your "Us"

May this book inspire you to take a look at your intimate connections. *The Book of US* is about preserving those key elements that make each relationship unique. It's about saying "thank you" to those who have chosen to share themselves with you. It's about celebrating your time together. It's about taking those familiar moments that bring us comfort and joy, and sharing them with others. It's about telling the stories of your "Us". Turn the page and let's get started.

Angie

P.S. Internet linked resources supporting each chapter of this book are available on my website. (See the last page for more information.)

There are several ways to use *The Book of US*:

1. Create a whole album. *Take an idea from the In Your Scrapbook sections in each chapter, and use it for the foundation, adding content from the prompts in that chapter, or throughout the book.*

2. Create a relationship album. *Use the different themes from each chapter to allow you to create an album emphasizing a variety of relationships, from family to romantic to friendship. You will have one scrapbook chronicling the greatest influences in your life.*

3. Add meaning to your current albums. *Use the ideas and prompts in this book to create individual layouts. Let this book color your journaling, emphasizing the relationship aspect of your subjects.*

4. Choose 5 to 10 prompts to share. *List them on a worksheet and have loved ones respond to them. Include their words on layouts.*

5. Create a gift album. *Check out the concepts offered in Chapter 10 for ideas. You can also take ideas or prompts from other chapters to use as the foundation for a gift album.*

MEMORIES

OF US

STIFT VORAU 50g

REPUBLIK ÖSTERREICH

TIME
Has taken the little girl
and left
in its place a...
YOUNG WOMAN...

1995

May 23, 1981—that's
when we met for the first
time. You were 4 days
old, and I'll never forget
how excited I was to drive
down to Hollister to meet
you...my first niece - your
mom was the first of us (5
siblings) to have a child.
I'm not sure if that's why
I still feel a special bond
with you, or if there's
another reason...but I

know that I've always felt
especially "connected" to
you. Even as you grew
older, and as children so
often do, wanted to spend
more time with your
friends than with your
family, that special
"connection" still re-
mains...You will always
be my "favorite girl!"

I love you!
Auntie

Once upon our time... this section encourages you to depict the history of a relationship. You could document a specific time period or cover the full timeline from meeting each other to present.

SUPPLIES: Tag album is 7Gypsies. Paper is Karen Foster, Mustard Moon, Rusty Pickle, Creative Imaginations, Pages in a Snap and ProvoCraft. Cardstock is Bazzill Basics and Making Memories. Fonts are Cure-Picture Show, 2Peas Flea Market, Autumn Leaves Highlight and Times New Roman. Stamps are PSX, All Night Media and Hampton Art. Inks are Ranger Industries and Tsukineko. Decorative scissors are Fiskars. Scrabble tiles are from the Parker Brothers game, Scrabble.

Memories of Us Tag Book
by Kathy Montgomery

For her oldest niece's upcoming college graduation, Kathy wanted to put together a meaningful album showcasing special memories she had of their relationship, starting with the day she was born. "Because I have so many photos of her," Kathy said, "I decided to concentrate on the early years and used a photo of her middle-school graduation to 'close' the album."

We sat side by side in the morning light and looked out at the future together.

—Brian Andres

We find comfort among those who agree with us—growth among those that don't.

—Frank A. Clark

The influence of each human being on others in this life is a kind of immortality.

—John Quincy Adams

This chapter on history was inspired by the album I made for my husband and his friend (mentioned in the Welcome section). In creating that album, I realized the value in documenting the history of a relationship, in sifting through the thousands of memories to get at the crux of a relationship.

I loved my husband's idea of sorting all those random memories into themes. For instance, he could have included multiple layouts on all the different computer systems and games they've owned over the years, along with the years spent studying them. Instead, he chose to compile them within a computer section, titled, "Geeks from the Get Go." Many of the memories of

your relationships could be sorted this way. Consider the themes my husband defined:

- ❑ Elementary school
- ❑ Sleepovers
- ❑ Common interests
- ❑ Movies
- ❑ Jobs as teens
- ❑ High school
- ❑ College
- ❑ Road trips
- ❑ Accomplishments
- ❑ Significant others
- ❑ Weddings
- ❑ Careers
- ❑ Families

Birthday Mini Album
by Laurianna Murray

This album celebrates a 10-year friendship. With all of the journaling hidden in interactive elements, Laurianna had plenty of room for photos and embellishing while also telling her stories. "I had such a blast doing it," confided Laurianna. "I was actually pretty excited that there were no page protectors... this gave me the freedom to make each page interactive and fun. Plus... I know how she is. If I didn't slow her down and make her take the time to read the journaling, she would blow right by it! It is so cool to be able to do something you love and give a gift of your heart and creativity. That made it so special for me too!"

5/22/04

you & me

Can I even count all the places we have traveled together!
- Sacramento
- Jamaica
- New Orleans
- Minneapolis
- NYC

and who knows where else the years will take us! Here's to many happy travels!

The world is a book, and those who do not travel, read only one page.
— St. Augustine

Reminisce

travels

THAT WAS THEN   THIS IS NOW

We didn't have much, but we sure had plenty.
—Sherry Thomas

Life isn't a matter of milestones but of moments.
—Rose Fitzgerald Kennedy

We're still not where we're going but we're still not where we were.
—Natasha Josefowitz

At the end of your life, you will never regret not having passed one more test, not winning one more verdict or not closing one more deal. You will regret time not spent with a husband, a friend, a child, or a parent.
—Barbara Bush

SUPPLIES: Mini album is Bazzill Basics. Paper and stickers are K&Co. Stamp is Hero Arts. Ink by Colorbox. Twill tape is All My Memories. Washer words are Making Memories. Lettering is Dymo Label Maker.

6/3/04

Can you believe how skinny we were - kids - no curves - what's that about. So much better now that we are women - just a few less curves now would be nice! Remember the "I'm not scared" tshirts. I found mine this week! We thought we were too cool - Oh wait because we were - are - and always will be!
I love you!
Lori —

That it will never come again is what makes life so sweet.
—Emily Dickinson

These are my daughters, I suppose. But where in the world did the children vanish?
—Phyllis McGinley

Though the past haunts me as a spirit, I do not ask to forget.
—Felicia Hemans

In this chapter I've included other examples of how you could illustrate a history. It also goes beyond the thematic approach to answer the questions:

- How did we get to this point?
- What decisions and experiences have put us on this road?
- Where has that road already taken us?

Why is this theme important?

Looking back over the memories you've created together helps remind you of the commitment you've made to each other. It reaffirms the investment you've made in getting to this point. You can look at the challenges and experiences you've faced together and remember how strong you are as a team.

Chronicling a history is also beneficial for other people in your life—your kids may wonder how you met your spouse or what you did with your best friend in high school. Your family may wonder how you overcame certain challenges or how you achieved certain milestones in your past. Your scrapbook can document those moments in your history.

Becoming Us
by Cindy Bentley-Johnson

In this layout, Cindy saves the precise moment she and her husband moved from a friendly "us" to a romantic "us".

Do you remember such a moment in your own history? Scrapbooking the history of a relationship can be personally rewarding. "I am loving that I am documenting stuff about US", Cindy says with a twinkle in her eye.

SUPPLIES: Paper is 7Gypsies and Real Life. Alphabet stickers are EK Success and Real Life. Font is Vintage Typewriter. Ribbon is Making Memories. Tag and paper donut are EK Success.

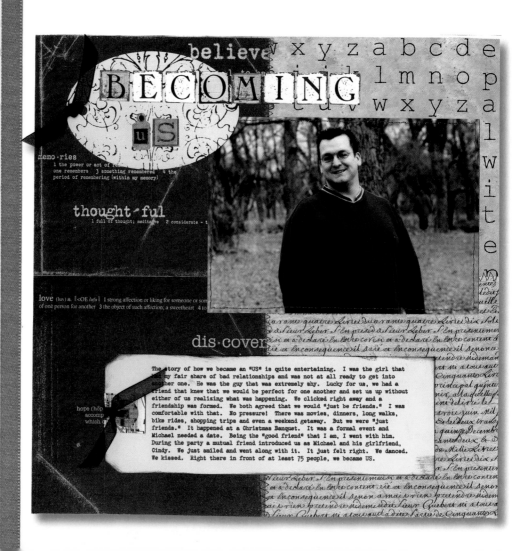

In your scrapbook...

There are any number of ways you could approach an album like this. You could do an actual timeline, detailing significant dates from the day you met, trips you took, weddings and other celebrations, through to present day. See Andrea Steed's (page 14) and Jennifer Papadimitriou's (pages 20 and 21) layouts for examples of this idea. Dana Swords' layout also demonstrates a way to present the highlights of years' of memories (page 18).

You could fashion an album of random memories, not grouped chronologically but in themes, like the album I created for my husband. Once you create a list of possible themes it may be easier to recall memories within each theme. Or, you can work in the opposite direction and brainstorm a list of memories and experiences you know you want to include and look for common themes among the memories. Then include a variety of memories on one layout for each theme (though you may need more than one layout to tell your stories).

Chronicle a specific time in your relationship, similar to London Stokes' engagement album (pages 22 and 23). She created calendar pages for each month of their engagement and used the calendar boxes for her

Time —our youth—it never really goes, does it? It is all held in our minds.
—Helen Hoover Santmyer

It doesn't happen all at once. You become. It takes a long time.
—Margery Williams

It is good to have an end to journey toward, but it is the journey that matters in the end.
—Ursula K. LeGuin

Butterflies & Fireworks
by Jennifer Harrison

"I just knew I'd meet a boy and those butterflies in my belly would never go away and there would be fireworks when we kissed. From the moment we met I knew I'd love you forever." And so began Jennifer's relationship with her husband. You can create a layout that illustrates your "butterflies & fireworks" by documenting how you met, what you liked about each other, and how you became an "Us". What makes you get butterflies in your belly?

Supplies: Paper is KI Memories and Kangaroo & Joey. Cardstock is Bazzill Basics. Rubber Stamps are Magenta and Making Memories. Ink is Stampin' Up. Font is Serifa th BT. Square black nails are Chatterbox.

Everyone is trying to accomplish something big, not realizing that life is made up of little things.

—Frank A. Clark

Love never gives up, never loses faith, is always hopeful, and endures through every circumstance.

—I Corinthians 13:7

Coming together is the beginning. Keeping together is progress. Working together is success.

—Henry Ford

journaling. You could do this kind of album or layout for any kind of countdown—counting down to a big vacation, a loved one returning home from the military, or the birth of a child. Be sure to include "real-life" ephemera like London did— phone bills, to-do lists, emails, etc.

Write about someone else's relationship, like Steph Stanley did for her great-grandparents (page 78). Journal what stories you know about them and their relationship. Then, add what you learned from observing their interactions.

Finally, scrap the milestones. Milestones aren't always positive accomplishments. A milestone is a significant or important event in somebody's life. Consider

documenting the challenges you've faced. Jami Myers' journaling talks about facing her husband's emergency triple bypass surgery and how that has affected their relationship (page 15). You could create layouts about time spent away from each other, unwise choices, unemployment or natural disasters. Always include journaling on how you made it through those times. That kind of journaling gives better understanding of who you are together.

Prompts to trigger journaling

❑ How did you meet? What were your first impressions of each other? What first drew you to each other? How have those impressions changed or confirmed?

SUPPLIES: Cardstock is Bazzill Basics. Stickers are Magenta. Fonts are Garamond and Carpenter. Eyelets are Making Memories. Quote is Scrapbook Magic by Fairy Tale Creations; poem by Jennifer O'Byrne.

Ben & Andrea, Through the Years
by Andrea Steed

Andrea created this 5x7 album to represent each year that she and her husband have been together. Each layout includes a photo and a list of highlights from the year. She likes it because "it's so easy to keep up!"

- Think for a moment. What were you doing one year ago? Five years ago? How have you both changed in that time? Consider using journal entries to go back and recall details. What additional information did your entry bring to mind?

- How do you make each other laugh? What private jokes have you had over the years?

- If you were to create a time capsule that would be opened in 20 years, what would you include in it? What would you write today to capture your life so in 20 years you would have a vivid picture of your relationship as it is today?

- What other people have crossed the path of your relationship? Describe the circumstances and the people.

- Where have you gone together? What out of town trips have you taken? List itineraries and include appropriate memorabilia.

- What challenges have you faced together? What mistakes have you made? What have you learned from them?

- Describe any turning points in your relationship. A turning point is a point at which a significant change occurs or one on which future developments depend.

For Today, Truly Blessed
by Jami Myers

It's not easy to scrap the scary times, but it can be powerful. In this layout, Jami documented one of the hardest challenges she and her husband faced in the history of their marriage, triple bypass surgery. When you scrap the hard things you've faced and survived, the layout becomes a testimony to the strength of your relationship. You don't need many photos — let your journaling tell the story.

SUPPLIES: Paper, frames and nails are Chatterbox. Cardstock and vellum are Bazzil Basics. Font is Liorah BT for journaling and hand cut title.

Love is what you've been through with somebody.
—James Thurber

❏ Compile a chronology of your relationship. Write each year of your relationship at the top of an individual piece of paper. Jot down events, highlights, trips, accomplishments and milestones for each year. Use those notes to create layout(s).

❏ Choose a word or phrase that sums up each year in your

relationship. Use that word or phrase as the basis of a layout. Include the word's definition on the layout.

❏ What are your habits together? How have you established a rhythm to interacting with each other?

❏ Choose a song that represents your history and use it as the

and the future holds...

Life's Mosaic
by Shannon Bruce

Shannon was able to include 24 photos on this layout, providing glimpses of one specific year in their relationship. She used the index print from Kodak to get the small pictures of the baby in the fold out section, and used the Sizzix square die to cut the larger mosaic squares. Just think of the memories you could capture if you could include 24 photos for each year of your relationship!

Supplies: Paper is Making Memories. Diecuts are Sizzix. Font is CK Print. Eyelets are Stampin' Up. Fibers are Adornments. Metal alphabet is Making Memories. Pen is Milky.

basis for an album. Put one line of the song on a separate layout and choose an appropriate photo. Journal about why this song is so appropriate to your history. Include factual details about each photo on the back of each layout.

❑ Choose songs that represent each year in your history and use them as the basis for a scrapbook project. Consider compiling the songs on to a CD and including the CD in the album. Or type out the lyrics in a light-colored font and use it as background paper.

❑ If you're documenting a romantic relationship, how and when did you know the other person was "The One"? How does the other person continue to be "The One"?

Photos to include

❑ Photo of each of you around the time that you met

❑ Photo of the place where you met (even if you have to go take the picture now)

❑ Photos depicting highlights of particular years

❑ Photos from trips you've taken together

Don't be dismayed at goodbyes. A farewell is necessary before you can meet again. And meeting again after moments or lifetimes is certain for those who are friends.
—Richard Bach

Love is a four-letter word spelled T-I-M-E.
—Unknown

We Did It!
by April Mensik

During their first year of marriage, April's husband traveled to Europe six times for work, often for three-week-long classes. It was not an easy time for either of them, being apart for that long. "We took turns being wimps!" wrote April. Scrapbooking about times when you miss each other illustrates how much you enjoy being together and how grateful you are when that happens. April's jubilant title and journaling says it all – "We did it! We survived! We made it!" What circumstances have you survived in the course of your relationship?

SUPPLIES: Paper is American Crafts. Stickers are Wordsworth.

People think they have to find their soulmate to have a good marriage. You're not going to "find" your soulmate... You get married, and after 20 years of loving, bearing and raising children, meeting challenges—then you'll have "created" your soulmate.

—Diane Sollee, smartmarriages.com

❑ Photos illustrating different hairstyles

❑ Photos taken yearly or in 5- to 10-year increments

Memorabilia to include

❑ Scans of CD covers for music you've listened to over the years

❑ Printouts of movie posters for movies you've enjoyed together

❑ Brochures from activities or causes you participated in together

❑ Menus from restaurants you frequent or where significant "relationship moments" have occurred

❑ Logos or mascots from schools or other groups you attended together

❑ Letters you wrote to each other

❑ Scans of fabric from significant clothes

The First Five Years
by Dana Swords

This layout features a file folder style booklet with a page that details highlights of each year of marriage. "When I showed this layout to my husband, he laughed so hard that he cried!" shares Dana.

Supplies: Paper is K&Co. Stickers are Rusty Pickle, Karen Foster and Making Memories. Fonts are Times New Roman, Arial, Rage Italic and Papyrus. Mesh is Magenta. Stamps are All Night Media. Ink is Stampin' Up. Fibers are Rub-a-Dub-Dub. Tack is Chatterbox. Charm is Card Connection. Ribbon is Offray.

Dear Dave,
It was November 1994 when we first met, as pen pals on AOL. You were 19, and I had just turned 17, a junior in high school. You know what I liked about your emails? You could spell and you had proper punctuation. I had never known anyone from New Hampshire before, and you seemed like a nice guy. We wrote emails to each other nearly every day, and got to know each other. In those days we talked about tv shows, music, school, and friends.

And so we remained pen pals for quite some time, until my senior year approached, and prom time! I did not have a date, so my friends came up with an idea to have you fly down to surprise me as my date! We met in person on April 26, 1996 as a huge surprise. I was SHOCKED and incredibly nervous.

Nov 11, 1994:	our first email on AOL
April 27, 1996:	we met in person at my prom
June 1, 1996:	I graduated from high school
August 1996:	your second trip to NC
1996-1999:	we continued emailing

Time passed
...and we remained email friends for several years, throughout our time at college. You had been working in the real world for 2 years before I even graduated. I went to Australia in 1999 and you were my rock during that time; I could always count on you for support. I'm not sure but I think it was while I was gone that I did a lot of thinking and came to the realization that when I looked back on the past 5 years YOU were the one who was always there for me, the one I was closest to and the one friend I never outgrew. We took a chance and I flew to NH as soon as I got back to the USA... and it worked! We were immediately in love. We began a long distance relationship, and flew back and forth to see each other every three months or so. It was so hard to be apart.

Feb-July 1999:	I was studying abroad in Australia
August 1999:	my first NH visit
October 1999:	2nd NH visit, went to Salem, Mass.
December 1999:	You gave me a gold necklace for my
March 2000:	3rd birthday, our first Christmas
May 2000:	we went to NH, our first Christmas
July 2000:	visit to NH; we went to Asheville NC together
November 2000:	you came for my graduation from UNC
February 2001:	we went to Ben & Jerrys in Vermont and Foxwoods in Connecticut
	Road trip to Charleston SC
	Valentine's Day at the Cheesecake

Love endures
If absence makes the heart grow fonder, we must have been the most head over heels couple in the world. The months of not seeing each other between visits became so painful that we knew something had to change. We endured a long distance relationship from 1999-2001 before I packed up and moved from North Carolina to New Hampshire to be together full time. It was the most heartbreaking decision I have ever had to make, and I still feel homesick even now. But we knew that we were meant to be together, so making a choice between my home and you was simply something that had to be done. Our first couple of months living together had some tense moments as I adjusted and tried to find work, but it was always evident that our love was growing stronger. Time heals all things and we loved being together.

June 1, 2001:	After driving 12 hours from NC we arrived in NH at my new home
June 3, 2001:	We adopted our first cat Dixie from the Bedford Animal Shelter
July-Sept 2001:	I had a horrible job at a kennel
Sept 2001:	I started working at Oxford

Sweet life
Eight months after I moved to NH, you proposed to me on the rocky beach of Fort Foster, Maine, on a cold but sunny February day. It was an incredibly happy day for both of us, and we had our whole lives ahead of us and a wedding to plan! But first, we had to buy a house. We had been renting an apartment for a year and decided that the sooner we bought a house, the better off financially we would be. The rest of 2002 was spent buying a home, moving, and getting settled in. Our engagement lasted twenty months, and we were married on the day of my 26th birthday. You were 28. And here we are. Not yet married a full year, but already like an old married couple. We love our little life in our little house with our cats, others sentences. We finish each and as always, each other. I love you, baby!

February 9, 2002:	we got engaged in Maine!
June 2002:	we bought our first house
October 2002:	we adopted our second cat JoJo from the Manchester Animal Shelter
Winter 2003-2003:	the worst winter in years in NH!
August 2003:	we adopted our third cat Moby
October 18, 2003:	we were married in Francestown, NH on a beautiful autumn day

10 Years of US *by Erika Follansbee*
These pages tell the story of how Erika and her husband met and later ended up together. The format of the pages is kept consistent to support the timeline. The upper half contains journaling in letter form along with recent pictures. The bottom half is for timeline information and old pictures relating to the timeline. Erika says, "I wanted to tell how far we've come together and to document what obstacles and events we've overcome to get where we are today."

SUPPLIES: Paper is Rusty Pickle, 7Gypsies and Me & My BIG Ideas. Font is 2Peas Renaissance, downloaded from www.twopeasinabucket.com. Embellishments are Making Memories.

10 Year Timeline & Anniversary
by Jennifer Papadimitriou

Jennifer used a panoramic page protector to make a 4-page spread that included this timeline. She documented key points in her relationship with her husband, starting back in 9th grade in high school, through celebrating 10 years together. The photos, cut and punched in squares and rectangles, help show the progression of their history together. On the title page for the timelines, she included some dried flowers from the anniversary bouquet in a memorabilia pocket.

T I M E

Sept. 1989	Jen notices Bob walk by in grade 9 for the first time. Thinks he's cute...
Oct. '89	Bob aggravates Jen in science class
Sept. 1990	Bob & Jen flirt with each other in typing class
April 1991	Bob declares he has a crush on her
May '91	Bob asks her to be his girlfriend! – 1st kiss!
May 10/91	Their first date at Reggies Restaurant in Barrie. Watch Toy Soldiers at Imperial 8 Cinemas (Jen's dad drives them!)
June 10/91	Bob decides he doesn't have time for a girlfriend and breaks up with her
1992	Bob calls Jen occasionally
May 1993	Bob starts calling on a regular basis
June '93	Decide to go on a "friend" date to see The Firm at Imperial 8 Cinemas. Jen desperately wants to hold his hand!
July 15, 1993	Bob comes over to visit and they decide to become a couple again! (Jen dumps her current boyfriend!)
August 20/93	They say "I love you" for the first time!
Christmas 93	Their first Christmas together!
May 28/1994	Prom Night!
June '94	Grade 12 Graduation
Sept.–June/95	Both stay in school to complete OAC's
Sept. 1995	Bob attends WLU University and moves to Kitchener. Jen works for a year in Barrie and they visit each other often
May 1996	They take a trip to Dominican Republic for two weeks!
Sept. '96	Bob goes back to school and Jen starts Humber College in Etobicoke
July 1998	Visit sunny Florida for two weeks!
Jan. 1999	Jen begins her internship at Chapters.ca as an Annotation Writer

SUPPLIES: Cardstock is Colormates. Punch is Marvy square punch. Typewriter stickers are Rebecca Sower Nostalgiques. Photo anchors are Making Memories. Black brads are Karen Foster.

June 2000	Bob and Jen both graduate from college/university
July '00	Jen is promoted to Full-Time Merchandise Coordinator at Chapters!
Aug. '00	Bob goes to Greece to try out for Pro-Basketball. Stays for 8 weeks! Decides not to stay.
Oct. 25/00	Bob is hired at Dell Computer as sales rep.
Nov. '00	Begin apartment hunting in Scarborough
Dec. '00	Move in Dec. 28th!
March 2001	Chapters merges, Jen gets laid off
April '01	Jen gets hired at Procuron as Research Analyst
July '01	Bob wins Sales Rep of Quarter and earns them a trip to Cancun on Sept. 19th!
Aug. '01	Bob buys an engagement ring! (without Jen's knowledge!)
Sept. 11/01	Disaster strikes for New York. All flights cancelled and trip postponed until November.
Nov. 16-23	Get engaged in Cancun on Nov. 17th!
Nov. 25/01	Jen gets laid off at Procuron and they decide to move back to Barrie
Jan. 31, 2002	Move into Bob's mom's house for a year to save money
Jan '02	Jen starts to plan the wedding!
April '02	Purchase their first home on Watson Drive in Barrie!
Nov. 17/02	Get Married at Fantasy Farm in Toronto!
Nov. 18-30	Honeymoon at Carriage Hills in Horseshoe Valley
Dec. 12/02	Move into their new home!
July 15, 2003	Celebrate their 10th anniversary together! Order Chinese food and snuggle at home!

L I N E

Engagement Monthly Album
by London Stokes

This 12x12 spiral bound book holds two-page layouts for each of the nine months London was engaged to her husband. She chose her cardstock based on her wedding colors and included a ladybug on each month's layout (a ladybug was the theme of their wedding). Each page features a photocopy of London's wedding planner calendar along with other images and journaling to describe activities from each month.

Can you think of time periods from your own relationships that could be documented using this calendar or time capsule approach?

SUPPLIES: *Title Page:* Fonts are LMS Lily of the Valley and CK Journaling. Time capsule information by C. K. Clips.

September & November: Fonts are CK Classic, CK Cursive, CK Rubber Pencil, Scrap Formal, CK Journaling, Times New Roman and LD Tall Pen.

June: Font are CK Classic, CK Cursive, Scrap Amor, LD Splash, Scrap Script and Scrap Map. Diecuts are My Minds Eye.

MEMORIES

November
nineteen ninety eight

registering

My family wanted us to get our registering done before Christmas. So we registered early in November. We tried to pick stores that carried what we liked and could be found outside of Utah. We registered for everyday things at Target, and our China, Crystal and Silver at ZCMI and Dillards.

Our Patterns

China: Christian Dior Casablanca
Crystal: Lenox Courtyard Gold
Silver: Wallace Golden Aegean Weave
Sewing Silver: Wilton Armetale Reggae

MONTH November 1998

S	M	T	W	T	F	S
						? registered @ Dillards
					Cindy's B-day!	

TARGET

Nikon 35MM Camera
19" TV/VCR
Sienna Plaid Comforter
Sienna Plaid Tailored Sham
Sienna Plaid Sham
Sienna Plaid Dust Ruffle
Sienna Plaid Tailored Pillow
Sienna Plaid Pleated Pillow
Wonderful Deluxe Pillow
White Down Pillow
Parchment Ivory Flat Sheet
Parchment Ivory Fitted Sheet
Expanda Grip Mattress Pad
Denim Tab Shower Curtain
Opulence Forest Bath Towel
Opulence Forest Hand Towel
Opulence Forest Washcloth
Opulence Forest Rug Contour
Opulence Forest 24x40 Rug
Wood & Metal Toothbrush Hold
Wood & Metal Soap Dish
Wood & Metal Tumbler
Wood & Metal Tissue Holder
Wood & Metal Wastebasket
Square Dance Table Runner
Potpourri Block Placemats
Potpourri Block Napkins
Potpourri Chair Pads
8pc Gala Black Set
5pc Airtaka Box Set
7pc Cobalt Bake Set
Softworks Serving Utensils
Black Oster Toaster Oven
Braun Power Steamer
Fantom Upright Vac
Scrub Devil
Food Steamer/Rice Cooker
Sunbeam Deep Fryer
Chefpro Food Process
Black High Back Chair
Black Folding Table
TV Table
Toshiba Cordless Phone
3 Pc Tilted Cookie Jars
Domino Clear Corker
Aluminum Trivet
Utensil Holder
Ultra File 2 Door
SJ pc Bmd Tool Set
Faria Global Flatware
Worldview Lapis Dinner Plate
Worldview Jade 6" SQ Platter
Worldview Ivory 7" Bowls
Worldview Onyx Mugs
Worldview Jade/Lapis S&P
Worldview Ivory SQ Platter
Worldview Ivory 10" Bowl
Worldview Jade 5" Bowls
Worldview Lapis Salad Plate
Over the Sink Rack

Dillards

Sterling Silver
Mikasa Paris Ivy Frame
Mikasa Safari 8" Vase
Mikasa Safari 7" Vase
Mikasa Safari 6" Fribowl
Mikasa Safari 11.5 Fribowl
Mikasa Safari 9" Bowl
Mikasa Safari 9" Bowl
Mikasa Safari CWB Box
Griddle Abing Tray
Giraffe Pitcher
W.K. Fretwork Oval Tray
Elephant Bowl 14"
Elephant Tray
Large Picture Bowl w/ Server
Reggae Large Round Tray
Reggae Sm Serving Bowl
Reggae 30z. Bowl
Reggae Wind Coaster
Reggae Brad Tray
Reggae Oval Tray
Reggae 20z. Squard Baker
Reggae 30z. Rect. Baker
Reggae Trivet
Reggae Pitcher
Reggae Chips & Dip

ZCMI

Courtyard And Beverage
Courtyard Wine Glass
Courtyard Flute
Parisian Ivy Vase 8.5"
Parisian Ivy Oval Relish Tray
Reggae Brad Tray
Reggae 30z. Rect. Baker
Reggae Large Oval Tray
Reggae Med. Round Tray
Reggae Chip & Dip
Reggae Large Round Tray
Reggae Serving Bowl
Reggae Trivet
Reggae Pitcher

June
nineteen ninety nine

The Final Countdown

We received most of our reply cards back before the deadline date of the 11th. Those we didn't hear from I called. In the end we had a headcount of 200 people, much more than we had guessed. We gave our final count to David so they could plan food & seating.

Bridal Shower Guests

London Myers
Linda White
Corinne Myers
Cynthia Jarvis
Christy Myers
Brenna Vaughn
MaryLou Thirkill
Martha Dykstra
Linda Stokes
Mary McGuivery
June Cummiskey
Marilyn Jensen

MONTH June 1999

S	M	T	W	T	F	S
					Reply's Back	Weather-to Bookbind
Final Count to David					Cindy left	Myers Bdal & Bridal Shower
				Bridesmaids luncheon		Cooke + Harmon wedding!!

Showered
With Love & Affection

On June 19th Corrine gave me a Bridal Shower. She planned all sorts of games and served a light lunch!
On June 24th I got together with a few of the Bridesmaids for a Bachelorette party of games & pedicures.
On June 28th, I treated my Bridesmaids and both "mems" to a luncheon at Maddox's.

Testing...1-2-3

We had a busy evening before the wedding. The whole bridal party met at Mom & Dads for a rehearsal. It was hot. I thought we were all going to melt. Everything went well...and then we all headed up to Sherwood Hills for a rehearsal dinner. Every member of the Bridal party and their family was invited, and nearly everyone came! At the dinner Darren & I gave the bridal party and our parents gifts. My Mom gave Darren a mug from my Dad. We also asked everyone to fill out prediction sheets about Darren & I. We won't open these until our 10 year anniversary!

Mr. and Mrs. Darren S. Stokes

Our Thank You Cards

...and Then We Were One...

Organizing the stories of your relationships into a book gets easier once you have a theme or approach. This chapter shows how to focus your Book of Us stories around a central idea or theme.

Supplies: Paper is Mustard Moon. Fonts are P22 Garamouche, CK Print and CK Cursive.

ABCs of Toni & Me
by Andrea Steed

Use the alphabet for the basis of a theme album. In this example, Andrea created "The ABCs of Toni & Me", based on their college years together and the importance of their friendship. "It's an easy way to organize a theme book and it worked perfectly for this album," confirms Andrea.

The ABC's

It's not what you do once in a while; it's what you do day in and day out that makes the difference.
—Jenny Craig

Sometimes it's the SMALLISH things that take up the most room in our hearts.
—Winnie the Pooh

Adventure is worthwhile in itself.
—Amelia Earhart

A theme album is one which is limited to a specific category of events or memories, some idea that unifies all the layouts in an album project. It's often created using a pre-determined style, layout and design. Theme albums tend to have a cohesive feel, a beginning and an end, and maintain consistent colors, pattern paper, and lettering or titles.

Theme albums typically include photos and memorabilia from just one common topic, rather than unrelated events along a timeline. This perspective allows you to see growth and development over the span of years.

A Book of Us theme album is great for capturing unique facets of your relationships. It encourages you to choose one aspect of your time together and fully explore it on the pages of your scrapbook. By choosing a specific theme, you can draw a picture of your relationship within this one aspect. Ask yourself, "How do we interact with each other in relation to..." whatever theme you choose. For example, ask yourself, "How do we interact with each other in relation to our values?" This will really help you focus on recording what's most important to you.

When making a theme album, it helps to have the same "look"

5 Words to Describe...

These pages are a part of a circle journal that Michelle, Kristy and Tracy worked on together (see Chapter 9 for more examples). For this project, Michelle chose individual layout topics, then each scrapper completed them about Michelle. You could do a variation on this with a "Five Words to Describe..." theme album. Think of different aspects of your relationship and then describe them in five words. You could provide the journaling yourself or ask each person in your "us" for their input on a variety of topics such as five words to describe us; to describe our hometown; to describe our faith; to describe our goals.

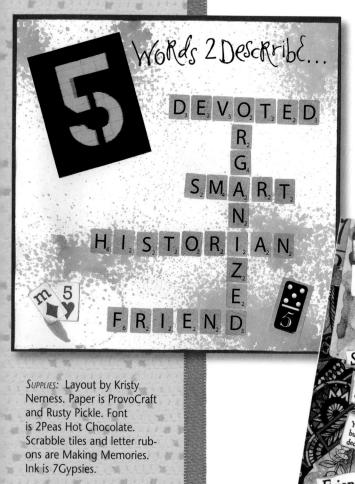

SUPPLIES: Layout by Kristy Nerness. Paper is ProvoCraft and Rusty Pickle. Font is 2Peas Hot Chocolate. Scrabble tiles and letter rub-ons are Making Memories. Ink is 7Gypsies.

The **ABC's**

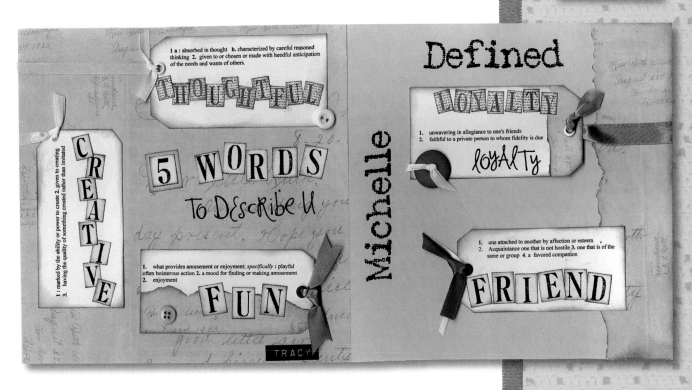

1 a : absorbed in thought b. characterized by careful reasoned thinking 2. given to or chosen or made with heedful anticipation of the needs and wants of others.

THOUGHTFUL

Defined

LOYALTY

1. unwavering in allegiance to one's friends
2. faithful to a private person to whom fidelity is due

loyAlTy

CREATIVE

1 : marked by the ability or power to create 2. given to creating often created rather than imitated
3. having the quality of something created rather than imitated

5 WORDS
TO DESCRIBE U

Michelle

1. what provides amusement or enjoyment; *specifically* : playful often boisterous action 2. a mood for finding or making amusement 3. enjoyment

FUN

1. one attached to another by affection or esteem
2. Acquaintance one that is not hostile 3. one that is of the same or group 4. a favored companion

FRIEND

TRACY

Supplies: Layout by Tracy Gossard. Paper is K&Company. Cardstock is Bazzill Basics. Rub-on letters are Making Memories. Label is Dymo.

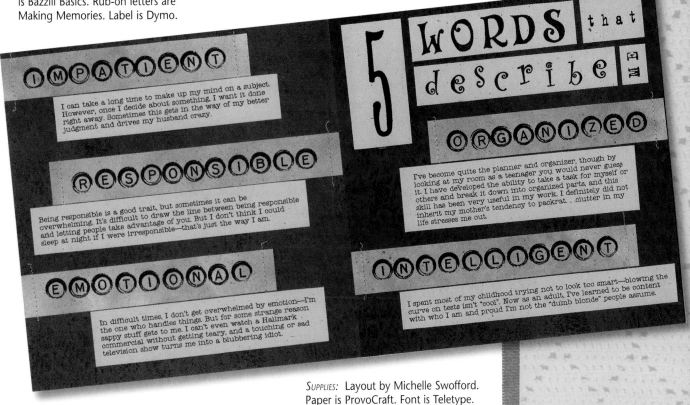

IMPATIENT

I can take a long time to make up my mind on a subject. However, once I decide about something, I want it done right away. Sometimes this gets in the way of my better judgment and drives my husband crazy.

5 WORDS that describe me

RESPONSIBLE

Being responsible is a good trait, but sometimes it can be overwhelming. It's difficult to draw the line between being responsible and letting people take advantage of you. But I don't think I could sleep at night if I were irresponsible—that's just the way I am.

ORGANIZED

I've become quite the planner and organizer, though by looking at my room as a teenager you would never guess it. I have developed the ability to take a task for myself or others and break it down into organized parts, and this skill has been very useful in my work. I definitely did not inherit my mother's tendency to packrat. . .clutter in my life stresses me out.

EMOTIONAL

In difficult times, I don't get overwhelmed by emotion—I'm the one who handles things. But for some strange reason sappy stuff gets to me. I can't even watch a Hallmark commercial without getting teary, and a touching or sad television show turns me into a blubbering idiot.

INTELLIGENT

I spent most of my childhood trying not to look too smart—blowing the curve on tests isn't "cool". Now as an adult, I've learned to be content with who I am and proud I'm not the "dumb blonde" people assume.

Supplies: Layout by Michelle Swofford. Paper is ProvoCraft. Font is Teletype. Stamps are Making Memories, Stampin' Up and Image Tree Nostalgiques.

The ABC's

throughout the book. This helps maintain consistency, and gives the album a sense of continuity, of being a "whole package" unto itself.

There are several ways to do this.

❑ You can choose one or two pieces of paper to use for borders through out the book. The borders can be different from page to page, but there is still a consistent look because the paper is the same.

❑ You could choose a family of papers, like papers within SEI lines all coordinated with each other. Then use those papers for the matting, for borders, for diecuts, for journal boxes, for titles. It really gives the book a consistent look.

❑ You could do all your layout titles the same way—like at the top left using the same rubber stamp alphabet. Or all lettering stickers. Or alternate top left with right

50 Days of Summer
by Tori Wools and Lauren Wools

"Last summer our goal was to do something different every day the girls were off, from the last day of school to the first," explains Tori. "Although we didn't get something done every day, we came close!" Tori and her three daughters made a point to sit down every other week and work on the album together. Tori gave her seven-year-old and nine-year-old several choices of paper to use; they picked what they liked best. Her five-year-old attached the photos, letter stickers and flowers herself. Not only did Tori's kids get to do lots of fun things on their vacation, they also were able to have a hand in preserving the memories themselves!

SUPPLIES: Paper is Making Memories. Stickers are Me & My Big Ideas. Diecut letters are Sizzix. Font is Girls are Weird. Paper piecing pattern from twopeasinabucket.com.

bottom, or down one side, then the other. All these things will be things that people will know to look for throughout the album.

Album Ideas & Memory Prompts

You could explore any number of topics in a Book of Us theme album. Consider these theme ideas:

❑ ABC Albums. The ABCs of Us, Wedding ABCs, Scripture ABCs

❑ The Colors of US. Almost like an ABC album, but with colors.
  o What does the color red make each of you think of?
  o How does red play into your shared memories?

❑ Favorite Family Recipes.
  o What are your family's favorite recipes?
  o What's on the menu for annual holiday dinners?
  o What foods do you enjoy fixing and eating together?

❑ The Dictionary of Us. Pick specific words, and pair them with appropriate photos, experiences, dreams, etc. Use either real dictionary definitions, or make up your own to better suit your relationship.
  o What words do you use that might not be in the dictionary?
  o What do you think should be added?

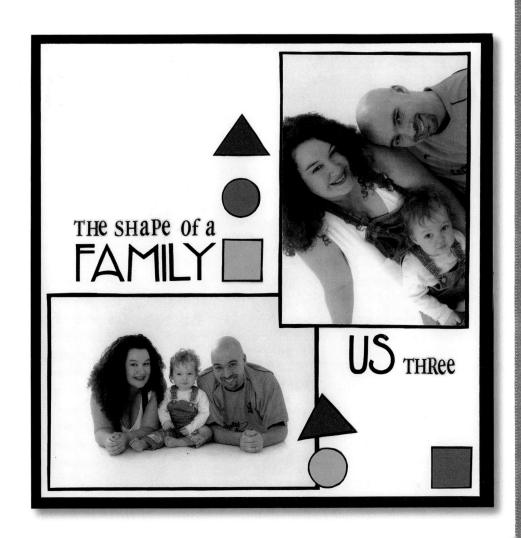

Love is not only something you feel. It is something you do."
—David Wilkerson

To say yes, you have to sweat and roll up your sleeves and plunge both hands into life up to the elbows.
—Jean Anouilh

Summer afternoon—summer afternoon; to me those have always been the two most beautiful words in the English language."
—Henry James

Shape of a Family
by Michelle Thompson

Consider making a theme album of photos from a professional portrait session, and using art to inspire the layout design. Michelle used Piet Mondrian's abstract art from the neoplastic period in the 1910s as the basis for these layouts. She appreciates having scrapped these photos because "this was one of the few opportunities we've had through the years to have photographs taken just of ourselves. Sometimes, with so much rush, rush, rush in this world, it is very easy to forget the most important relationship I have in my life."

SUPPLIES: Stickers are Me & My Big Ideas and Mary Engelbreit. Fonts are Impact and Bimini. Photo is by Venture Photography Studios.

The
ABC's

❑ Our Vacation Memories.
   o What seems to happen on every vacation?
   o What similarities can you find among trips over the years?
   o What are the necessary components of a road trip for your "us"?

   o What foods have you found on travels together? Include journaling on how each recipe "feeds" into your relationship.
❑ Our Memory Triggers.
   o What things, sounds, sights, and/or smells trigger memories of your "us"?

Being a Chronicle of alana's adventures in Housekeeping

Homemaking is unique in combining the most menial jobs with the most meaningful tasks....

Dorothy Patterson.

A Chronicle of Alana's Adventures & Power of Routines
by Alana Wylie-Reeves

Chores (opposite page)
by Holle Wiktorek

Think about chronicling your family's routines in a theme album. "All about us, is all about housekeeping!" says Alana. "Housekeeping is a way to take care of my family. A shiny sink is symbolic of my care for them." Journal about the way your family approaches housekeeping. Are you methodical or by-the-seat-of-your-pants? List out the chores for which each member of your family is responsible. "Library pockets are a great way to hold lists, especially 'to-do' lists!" Alana suggests. Holle's "Chores" layout illustrates another way to list out each person's chores, as well as their shared tasks. She even included pictures of them working on their tasks!

SUPPLIES: Pattern paper, buttons and tags are SEI. Stickers are SEI, Creative Imaginations, Lil' Davis, Me & My BIG Ideas and ProvoCraft. Snaps, staples and floss are Making Memories. Fonts are Abadi Condensed Light and Times Roman. Punches are Marvy Uchida.

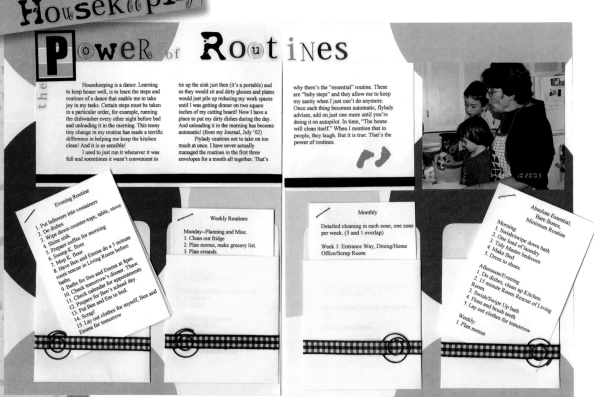

The Power of Routines

Housekeeping is a dance. Learning to keep house well, is to learn the steps and routines of a dance that enable me to take joy in my tasks. Certain steps must be taken in a particular order, for example, running the dishwasher every other night before bed and unloading it in the morning. This teeny tiny change in my routine has made a terrific difference in helping me keep the kitchen clean! And it is so sensible!

I used to just run it whenever it was full and sometimes it wasn't convenient to tie up the sink just then (it's a portable) and so they would sit and dirty glasses and plates would just pile up reducing my work spaces until I was getting dinner on two square inches of my cutting board! Now I have a place to put my dirty dishes during the day. And unloading it in the morning has become automatic! (from my Journal, July '02)

Flylady cautions not to take on too much at once. I have never actually managed the routines in the first three envelopes for a month all together. That's

why there's the "essential" routine. These are "baby steps" and they allow me to keep my sanity when I just can't do anymore. Once each thing becomes automatic, flylady advises, add on just one more until you're doing it on autopilot. In time, "The house will clean itself." When I mention that to people, they laugh. But it is true. That's the power of routines.

Evening Routine
1. Put leftovers into containers
2. Do dishes
3. Wipe down counter-tops, table, stove
4. Shine sink.
5. Prepare coffee for morning
6. Sweep K. floor
7. Mop K. floor
8. Have Ben and Emma do a 5 minute room rescue in Living Room before baths.
9. Baths for Ben and Emma at 8pm.
10. Check tomorrow's dinner. Thaw.
11. Check calendar for appointments
12. Prepare for Ben's school day.
13. Put Ben and Em to bed.
14. Scrap!
15. Lay out clothes for myself, Ben and Emma for tomorrow

Weekly Routines
Monday--Planning and Misc.
1. Clean out fridge
2. Plan menus, make grocery list.
3. Plan errands.

Monthly
Detailed cleaning in each zone, one zone per week. (5 and 1 overlap)

Week 1: Entrance Way, Dining/Home Office/Scrap Room

Absolute Essential, Bare Bones, Minimum Routine
Morning:
1. Swish/swipe down bath
2. One load of laundry
3. Tidy Master bedroom
4. Make Bed
5. Dress to shoes.

Afternoon/Evening
1. Do dishes, clean up Kitchen.
2. 15 minute Room Rescue of Living Room.
3. Swish/Swipe Up bath
4. Floss and brush teeth
5. Lay out clothes for tomorrow

Weekly:
1. Plan menus

o Document the stories of heirlooms, colognes, books, clothing, recipes and other memorabilia that bring memories of times spent together rushing back.

o What books do you read over and over?

o Do a mini-album of favorite stories you've read together, and include scans of the covers.

❑ Things that Make Us Laugh.

o What jokes, movie lines or words from your Dictionary of US make you laugh?

❑ Our Book of Values. Create pages on different character traits, such as courage, faith, listening, service, love, etc, then document examples of each trait shown by each person in your relationship.

❑ Our Daydreams. You could take this further and create a Dream album.

o List out each person's individual dreams, or your dreams to accomplish together.

o Leave journaling space to note when the goal is accomplished.

❑ Scriptures of Strength and Comfort. Choose scripture verses that bring each of your comfort and pair it with appropriate photos, experiences and dreams.

o What experiences have you had that you can attribute to a higher power?

o Write out some family prayers.

The ABC's

There is no pleasure in having nothing to do; the fun is having lots to do and not doing it.
—Mary Wilson Little

Jump into the middle of things, get your hands dirty, fall flat on your face, and then reach for the stars.
—Joan Curcio

I have only to take up this or that to flood my soul with memories.
—Dorothée DeLuzy

Life is no brief candle to me. It is sort of a splendid torch which I have got hold of for a moment, and I want to make it burn as brightly as possible before handing it on to future generations.
—George Bernard Shaw

SUPPLIES: Paper and fasteners are Chatterbox. Diecut tags are QuicKutz. Stamps are River City Rubber Works and La Pluma. Punches are EK Success. Paint is Apple Barrell. Pens are Krylon, EK Success and Sakura. Mesh is I luv scrapbooking.

The ABC's

- o Where did you learn them?
- o What do you do together that fulfills your spiritual needs?
- o Create a page of meaningful parts of church bulletins.
- o What have you experienced together that contributed to increasing faith to trust a person, or new skill or tool? You could take a religious angle, or look at everyday things.

- o What do you do to keep your hope alive?
- ❏ Letters Between Us.
  - o Use letters written between you to document time spent apart.
- ❏ A Slice of Our Life. Document the little everyday things that make up your life together.
  - o What are your schedules, routines, chore distribution, typical weekend activities?

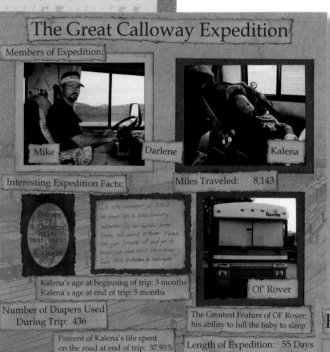

The Great Calloway Expedition
by Darlene Johnson Calloway

Darlene created a theme album of her family's "sea to shining sea" vacation. "When my daughter was just three months old," she says, "we loaded up our RV and visited our entire family from Florida to Ohio to Montana to Washington. We traveled over 8000 miles." Her layout was inspired by the Lewis & Clark Expedition book. "In their book," she explains, "they made notations of the amount and types of food they brought, their supplies and such. So I included the same interesting facts for our trip. These two pages are the opening pages for our trip across country."

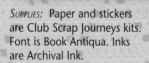

Supplies: Paper and stickers are Club Scrap Journeys kits. Font is Book Antiqua. Inks are Archival Ink.

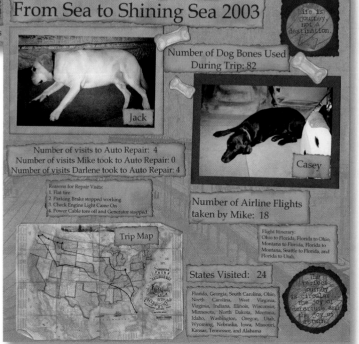

This was one of those days when we needed a photographer, so we could both be in the same photo! When we saw the state line sign, we had to pull in someone's yard to park and get the photograph. I guess we should have asked them! (I am sure it has been done before!) We didn't spend much time in Rhode Island, just a state line visit because we were trying to get to Washington, D.C. before too late in the evening. It took us a while to find a sign, even on the interstate, and there were no postcards to be found either. In fact, no one could understand my southern accent when I asked for the postcards. They asked me to repeat myself and then gave up on trying to help me!

SUPPLIES: Cardstock and vellum is DMD. Font is CK Primary. Letter stickers are Stickopotamus. Stencil is Wordsworth. Wire is Artistic Wire. Sequins and nail heads are JewelCraft. Chalk is Craf-T.

SUPPLIES: Paper and Scrapbook Times. Cardstock is DMD. Font is Typist. Diecut letters are QuicKutz. Stamps are La Pluma and Hero Arts. Punch is EK Success. Wire is Artistic Wire. Brads are Creative Impressions. Adhesive is Therm O Web.

50 States in 20 Years
by Holle Wiktorek

Create a theme album of the travels you've made together. Early in their marriage, Holle and her husband set a goal to visit all fifty states before their 20th anniversary. "We have reached 23 states so far," she says. "We try to get a photo of us by the state line sign, so we go to a Welcome Center or on a rural road and look for the sign." She also includes photos and journaling of other sites they see in each particular state. You could create a similar album, including Welcome Center brochures, and journaling about what stood out the most to each of you about each destination.

While being stationed at Ft. Bragg, North Carolina, we lived in Fayetteville. Raleigh, Wilmington, and Wrightsville Beach were also planned trips during our short stay. We lived in a nice neighborhood, and I enjoyed shopping while Thomas attended school. We were happy to be stationed there with our friends, Dave and Ann Ice. A favorite memory was celebrating my thirtieth birthday in this state.
June 2002-October 2002

SUPPLIES: Paper is hand painted. Stencil is Chatterbox. Cardstock is DMD. Font is CK Primary. Pens are EK Success and Sakura.

Once Thomas, Harley, Gracey, and I entered New Jersey, we stumbled across a High Point State Park for our dogs and Thomas to explore. They climbed, ran, and jumped on the rocks while I enjoyed the entertainment. After realizing New Jersey is called "The Garden State," we paid more attention to the produce stands, gardens, and livestock as we continued driving the backroads of the beautiful state.

The ABC's

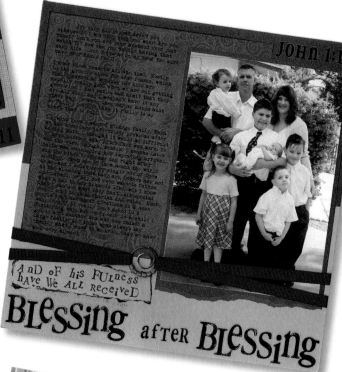

Scripture ABC
by Jennifer Wellborn

Here's another way to use the ABCs as the basis for a theme album. Jennifer chose keywords in alphabetical order, then paired them with appropriate scripture verses, meaningful journaling and photos of her family. The end result: Character lessons for her children, as well as a glimpse of what those values mean to her family.

Supplies: A: Paper is Chatterbox and Paper Patch. Font is Mom's Typewriter.

B: Paper is Mustard Moon. Font is Mom's Typewriter. Metal frame is Making Memories.

C: Paper is Scrappin' Dreams. Stickers are Me & My Big Ideas. Font is Mom's Typewriter. Stamp is Hero Arts. Ribbon is Wrights. Clip is Clipiola. Beads are Scrappin' Fools.

D: Paper is KI Memories. Stickers are Me & My Big Ideas. Font is Mom's Typewriter. Tacks are Chatterbox. Ink is Close to My Heart.

o Paint a picture of what your daily life together is like.

Photos to include

❑ Pictures of each of you doing one of your chores

❑ Pictures from trips you've taken together

❑ Pictures of furniture, clothes or other possessions that trigger memories

❑ Pictures of prepared recipes of family favorites

❑ Pictures of things that make you laugh

The ABC's

Normal day, let me be aware of the treasure you are. Let me learn from you, love you, bless you before you depart. Let me not pass you by in quest of some rare and perfect tomorrow. Let me hold you while I may, for it may not always be so. One day I shall dig my nails into the earth, or bury my face in the pillow, or stretch myself taut, or raise my hands to the sky and want, more than all the world, your return.

—Mary Jean Iron

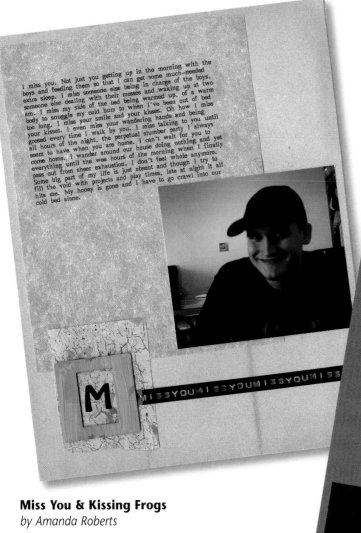

I miss you. Not just you getting up in the morning with the boys and feeding them so that I can get some much-needed extra sleep. I miss someone else being in charge of the boys. someone else dealing with their messes and waking up at two am. I miss my side of the bed being warmed up. of a warm body to snuggle my cold bum to when I've been out of bed too long. I miss your smile and your kisses. Oh how I miss your kisses. I even miss your wandering hands and being goosed every time I walk by you. I miss talking to you until all hours of the night. the perpetual slumber party I always seem to have when you are home. I can't wait for you to come home. I wander around our house doing nothing and yet everything until the wee hours of the morning when I finally pass out from sheer exhaustion. I don't feel whole anymore. Some big part of my life is just absent and though I try to fill the void with projects and play times. late at night it all hits me. My honey is gone and I have to go crawl into our cold bed alone.

M   MISSYOUMISSYOUMISSYOUMISS

Before I started to date, I was told I would have to kiss a lot of frogs before I found a prince. Lucky me, I skipped the frog part and found my prince on the first try. I didn't realize how special my relationship with you was until I started talking to other people. I can fully appreciate you now more so then before. We both never had another relationship and we both have never kissed other people. I can't even begin to think of life without you Toad because it's always been the two of us, out in the world trying to make it in life and having each other as support. I dread you deploying and I had to stop listening to the news because my heart aches for those women that have lost their husbands. I can' not begin to imagine what I will do without you. How will I sleep at night knowing you are so far away from home and being shot at while having to eat M.R.E.'s and sleep in some tent. It makes my heart ache. So for now, I'll kiss my prince and appreciate you every chance I get. Hopefully that will be enough to get me through the nights you are gone and I lay awake in our bed alldone.

I love you my prince.

Miss You & Kissing Frogs
by Amanda Roberts

Amanda created these layouts in letter form to express her thoughts about her husband's deployment. Her journaling candidly reflects her concerns and worries, what she misses about him, but most of all, her love for him. How can you use letters to illustrate what it was like to be apart from someone you love?

SUPPLIES: Paper, cardstock and vellum is by Club Scrap. Font in Miss You is Adhawin-Tamil. Title font in Kissing Frogs is TwoForJuanNF. Journaling font is Calligraph421 BT.

The ABC's

Memorabilia to include

- ❏ Maps or brochures from vacations or road trips
- ❏ Scans of book covers
- ❏ Printouts of routines or daily schedules
- ❏ Recipe cards
- ❏ Scans of letters or notes written during periods of absence
- ❏ Scans of heirlooms, such as jewelry or quilts, or other "memory triggers"

A Story about Grandma Quackenbush and Me

Stella Evelyn Allen was born January 11, 1903 and she married Stanley Paul Quackenbush when she was eighteen years old. They lived in and around Bedford, Indiana the first part of their lives. She gave birth to two daughters, Norma Evelyn and Betty Lou, my mother. After I was born, we lived with Grandma for a year. I called her "Maw-maw" then, as I wasn't exactly which one of the doting women my mother really was. She and my mother played with me all day, gave my golden locks a permanent wave when I was six months old, fussed with my hair and my clothes, and took me shopping to show me off. They liked to think I was a little Miss Sunbeam look-alike. I was spoiled beyond belief when we moved to our own house. My Pop and my Dad did their share of spoiling, too, but it was Grandma that always took my side, never made me cry, always comforted any tears I had, even as an adult. I grew up, married, and moved to Tennessee. After my Pop died, Grandma spent several weeks each summer with my family. We talked until late at night, crafted, knitted, crocheted, picked garden produce and canned it, painted, extracted honey from my beehives, cooked, sewed, read, watched the soaps (I always had to watch hers, however) and laughed until our sides hurt. We cried together watching Little House on the Prairie. My kids thought we were nuts most of the time, but they looked forward to her visits. Her many stories of the "old days" had entertained me all my life, and now my children were sitting at her feet listening to them as my siblings, my cousins, and I had done. Sadly, her memories of many things left her, and she died of Alzheimer's disease August 17, 1990. I have missed her every day she has been gone. This book is a collection of things that belonged to Grandma and of things in my life that remind me of her.

~Nancy Diane Walker, August 1, 2004

The Old Figurines

My favorite cousin, Lana, and I used to play with these old figurines during our visits to Tell City, Indiana. Grandma seemed to trust us with them. I never knew the value of them, but I think their value was great to Grandma. I believe Pop bought them for her for some special occasion, perhaps even an anniversary. Lana and I visited Grandma and Pop for a week in the summer and another week during our Christmas break from school. Our days were filled with fun and games that Grandma would encourage or initiate. She encouraged us to make up stories about the figurines. Of course, all of us were incurable romantics, so the stories were always Cinderella-type ones. We loved the handsome prince and the beautiful young maiden chosen by him. Or the figurines were always on their way to a dance or a masquerade party. Grandma would tell us about the lives and times of people who wore clothes like the figurines were wearing. She was always reading, and she loved books containing historical facts. When I reach up on the shelf to get these favorite old pieces, I hold them in my hands and gently handle them like I used to as a little girl. Perhaps I may even dream that I found my Prince Charming in my dear husband, and he certainly looks more handsome than this figurine. It definitely takes me back to my childhood and those carefree days of fun and imagination.

The Old Button Box

Grandma's button box held treasures dear to us all. On dreary, cold days in winter or rainy days in summer, she would get out the button box and let us choose a button. We would then play "Button, button, who's got the button?" Sometimes we would simply play with the buttons and tell tales of the older buttons' origin. Buttons that came off Pop's old shirts, Grandma's old coats, buttons from baby clothes made for us or for our mothers all found a place in Grandma's button box. We loved to run our fingers through the cold, smooth buttons. It was a sensation I have never forgotten, nor have I outgrown the feeling it invokes in me. To this day, when I need to replace a lost button, running my fingers through her buttons looking for the perfect one takes me back to long beautiful days spent with Grandma.

Grandma and I
Age Eighteen

Grandma and I each fell in love with our own Prince Charming when we were still in our teens. Grandma and Pop set a wonderful example to Dick and me about how to stay in love way into your old age. Their love was one of intensity that never seemed to wane as they aged. They became closer as the years went by. Dick and I are finding our love to be the same as theirs, never-ending, happily ever after, true love, hopelessly devoted to each other, best friends, golfing buddies, dinner companions, and fellow Christians with God at the center of our relationship.

The heart that loves is ever young.

-Greek Proverb

grandmother

granddaughter

The Story of Grandma & Me
by Nancy Walker

Nancy created this album as a "memory triggers" album. She found items around her house that made her think of her relationship with her grandmother. She took close-up photos of each thing and journaled anecdotes and memories related to them. This kind of album not only documents the heirlooms found in one's home, but also many snippets of seemingly random memories, now tied together by family treasures.

One particularly neat feature of this album is her button shaker box. Nancy scanned the contents of her grandma's button box and used that as the background of her shaker box. Then she included actual buttons as the shaker pieces. She scanned the button box lid and adhered it to a CD for the hinged cover for her shaker box.

SUPPLIES: Album is sarabook kit from Hot Off the Press. Paper is Hot Off the Press and Anna Griffin. Cardstock is Scrappapers. Fonts are Times New Roman and CAC Camelot. Stamp by Club Scrap. Inks by Ranger and Close To My Heart. Punch by McGill. Stickers by K&Company and Jolee's. Adhesive is Glue Dots.

The ABC's

Love 10x Over

Ten little fingers held tightly in mine.
Our loving marriage… years together are nine.
Eight million memories, more still to come.
Seven days a week. love fills our home.

Love 10x Over
by Emily Irwin

Consider using a poem as the basis for a theme album. The poem could be one of your favorites, or one you've written yourself, like this example from Emily. "I wrote this simple ten-line poem that captured the essence of the many reasons I love my incredible husband and two wonderful children," explains Emily. "For each layout I used one line of the poem and included a photo which is representative of that line from the poem. Additionally, there is hidden journaling for each layout that goes deeper to explain how this line applies to my life with my three heroes and just how much I love them."

SUPPLIES: Paper is Chatterbox and Creative Imaginations. Fonts are CK Elegant and PC Sommerset. Page flips, eyelets and brads are Making Memories. Rhinestones are Westrim. Conchos are ScrapWorks.

Six caring eyes look deep in my heart.

Sharing five thankfuls each night in the dark.

Four arms giving hugs, no words left to say.

Three gorgeous smiles always brighten my day.

Two precious angels I truly adore.

One awesome family… who could ask for more?

—Emily Irwin

The
ABC's

This special album is dedicated to three of the most wonderful children in the world. Noelle, David Jr., and Matthew. The entire time it was being created, you three were the thoughts in our minds with each entry. When we got stumped about what to put next, we would ask ourselves "what will the kids want to know about us?" Then, suddenly, we would remember another tidbit to add.

It was a bit hard to not keep it all super-happy. I found it hard to list some of the less flattering entries (such as we would talk about divorce) but we both felt it was important for you to see that while overall our lives are VERY WONDERFUL, we have had hard times. But we have endured those hard times and without them, we would not be who we are.

So, here we dedicated this album to the three of you. Some of the entries may seem small and insignificant, but we want you to know that each entry holds a little piece of us. We want you to always remember who we are and who we were. We hope that this 100 things about us will help keep the memories from fading. We love you, Love Mom & Dad

May 2004

1. The first time David saw me was in 1997 at a Victor Valley High School football game -- I didn't know he saw me.

2. His friend, Mark Burnett, pointed me out to David because I was someone who had a crush on Mark.

3. David told Mark that I was an "amazon" -- because I was so tall.

4. The first time I saw David was in the summer of 1988 and he was in his car (1988 Subaru Justy) with his friend Mark.

5. I thought David had beautiful blue eyes -- they were actually colored contact lenses and his eyes are brown.

6. David and I became good friends after we met.

7. In 1989, I went with David and one of his friends to Castle Amusement Park in Riverside, CA. We were just friends.

8. We played miniature golf.

[...] and I also went to Silverwood Lake for swimming, where I [...] nk and black bathing suit.

David asked me to be hi[...]

31. I began attending Victor Valley College in 1991.

32. I began teaching preschool in 1992. We started becoming more financially sta[...]

33. We lo[...] barbecue. Our favorites to cook are burgers and steaks.

34. I love baked potatoes, but David would rather have French fries.

35. We both like salads, but David prefer bleu cheese dressing and I prefer Thousand Island.

36. We both love movies -- especially those that are full of suspense.

37. David and I were both born in California. Baldwin Park for him, and Santa Barbara for me.

38. We both came from low income families, but hid it from each other when we first starting dating.

39. We were both very jealous in the early years of our [...]

40. But as the years went on, we learned that th[...] jealousy [...]

11. I happily agreed.

12. On July 17, 1989, David and I kissed for the first time.

13. It was the best kiss I had ever had.

14. David and I moved in together in August of 1989.

15. In September 1989, we found out I was pregnant with Noelle.

16. Noelle was born on June 26, 1990 via c-section in Pomona, CA

17. We were married on August 5, 1990 in Las Vegas, NV at the Candlelight Wedding Chapel.

18. Our first apartment was in Adelanto, CA and we paid $350 per month.

19. Times were rough and we never had a lot of money.

20. We fought a lot.

100 Things About Us
by Brandie Valenzuela

With help from her husband, Brandie created this theme album for her three children. "The entire time it was being created, they were the thoughts in our minds with each entry," Brandie says. "When we got stumped about what to put next, we would ask ourselves: 'what will the kids want to know about us?'" In her dedication, she writes, "We want you to always remember who we are and who we were. We hope that this '100 things about us' will help keep the memories from fading." What 100 things can you come up with to help someone understand your "us" better?

SUPPLIES: Album is Making Memories. Journaling font is Helvetica. Ribbon is Offray.

Table of Contents

Fuchsia — Dedication

Red — Remember When

Orange — Ways We Are Alike

Gold — Favorite Family Tradition

Yellow — Things I Like About You

Chartreuse — Things We Agree/Disagree On

Green — Spring & Summer, Fall & Winter

Turquoise — Memories of Home

Blue — Feelings

Purple — Unanswered Questions

Our perspectives: 3

Most relationships are a combination of similarities and opposites. This chapter helps you compare and contrast your "Us" by presenting each person's response to different topics.

SUPPLIES: Paper is Hot Off the Press and ProvoCraft. Fonts are DisneyPrint and Walt Disney.

She Said, She Said
by Hannah Means

This album puts the phrase, "Like Mother, Like Daughter" to the test. Hannah wrote a list of questions that she sent to her daughter to answer. She answered the same questions before she saw her answers. They also have a page for unanswered questions—how wonderful that they are addressing these *now*, while answers are still available!

In every person who comes near you look for what is good and strong; honor that; try to imitate it, and your faults will drop off like dead leaves when their time comes.
—John Ruskin

There is no end. There is no beginning. There is only the infinite passion of life.
—Frederico Fellini

Blessed is the influence of one true loving human soul on another.
—George Eliot

You're Just Like Your...
by Kristin Baxter

Lists pointing out similarities help children feel a sense of identity and belonging within your family. Kristin used bullet-point journaling here to show the similarities her son shares with his mother and father. Bullet-point lists make journaling easy. Just jot down key points—you don't even have to worry about writing in complete sentences. This layout design would also be easy to recreate—a photo enlargement, a few strips of cardstock run through the printer, and boom, you're done!

SUPPLIES: Cardstock is Bazzill Basics. Title fonts are Arial Black and 2Peass Mr. Giggles (downloaded from www.twopeasinabucket.com); journaling font is Whackadoo.

The most valuable thing you bring to any relationship is yourself. In the process of involving yourself in a relationship, you are contributing your history, your thoughts, your goals, and your unique perspective, just as the other person contributes theirs'. All this significantly affects the relationship and affects the growth of each person in the relationship. It's the interplay of all these factors that makes the relationship interesting, and ultimately what makes a relationship work or not work.

Take the time to catalog those things that you have in common and those things that make you unique. Answer the question, "Who are these people who make this 'Us'?"

Describe the points where you find common ground, as far as tastes, ideologies, viewpoints, and habits, as well as how you differ from each other.

For this kind of Book of US, I suggest you pick a topic, prompt or question and pose it to each person. There's any number of ways you could approach this.

❑ You could pick a topic such as your favorite way to spend a Saturday afternoon and pose it to the other person in your relationship or each person in your group. Then scrap the responses along with your own.

❑ You could make a topical list of favorites, like a movie, color,

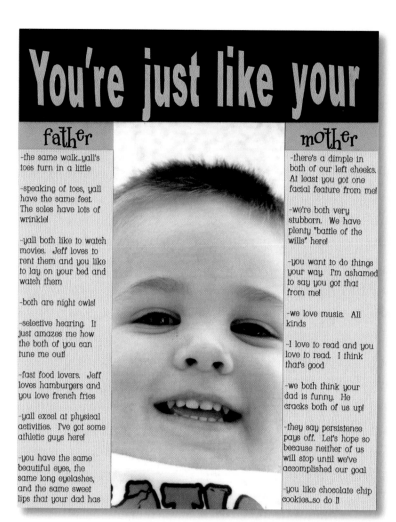

food, number, book, restaurant, etc, and include responses.

❑ You could also do a page featuring journaling on a specific event, but from each person's point of view, such the first time you met.

The point is to show how you are alike and different. Highlight how those similarities and differences play and feed off each other and how they affect your relationship. What do you appreciate about them? What have you learned because of these factors? How do the other person's strengths feed you? How do your perspectives, ideologies, strengths and weaknesses balance each other in the relationship? What differences have posed challenges for you?

Why is this theme important?

By describing the similarities and differences in your perspectives, you paint a portrait of you as individuals—people who have chosen to come together to make an "Us". In the process, you will have the opportunity to get to know the other person better. It's a chance to recognize and appreciate all that you both contribute to the relationship.

In your scrapbook...

Create an album of "My Favorite Memory" and include responses from each member. Encourage each person to include specifics on where and when the memory took place, and what they liked best. You could also include a list of "Honorable Mentions" at the back of the album,

My Boys
by Kacie Liechty

This layout lists the many similarities between Kacie's husband and son. Notice how she not only journaled each description on strips of paper, but also wound each strip with embroidery floss. This is a great way to add meaningful content to everyday photos. She could have simply titled the layout, "My Boys", but instead chose to draw some comparisons between their personalities.

SUPPLIES: Paper is Carolee's Creations. Cardstock is Bazzill Basics. Letter stickers are Karen Foster Design. Fonts are 39Smooth and Steamer. Eyelets and tag are Making Memories. Chalk is Craf-T. Floss is DMC.

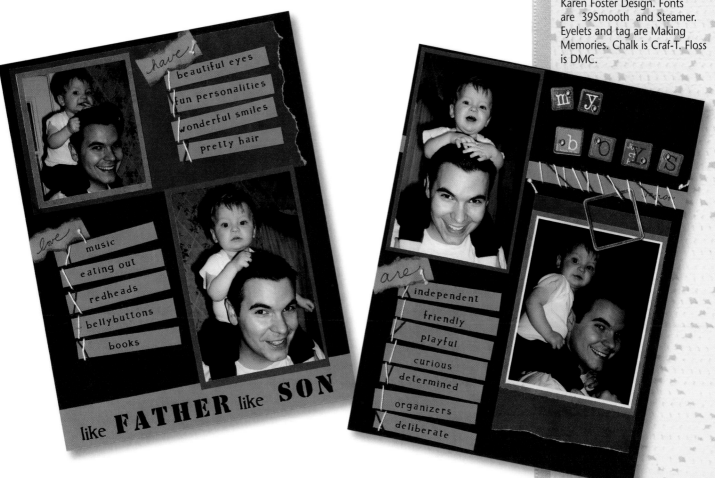

When you come right down to it, the secret of having it all is loving it all.

—Dr. Joyce Brothers

Live with wolves, and you learn to howl.

—Spanish proverb

Each one sees what he carries in his heart.

—Johann Wolfgang Von Goethe

Sometimes I think I should just keep my opinions to myself, she said, but someone has got to be the voice of reason.

—Brian Andreas

In His Eyes
by April Mensik

Here's a twist on a perspective layout: April's journaling reflects how she believes her husband views her; these words reveal an "invincible" woman, "silly, fun loving, and carefree!" Couldn't we all use a little dose of how our loved ones see us, instead of our critical inner eye? What a powerful exercise, to force yourself to try to see how your loved ones see you, then journal it in your own words.

SUPPLIES: Paper is Chatterbox. Stickers are Doodlebug. Stamps are Hero Arts. Cardstock is Bazzill Basics.

listing other memories that you all agree were great, but didn't make the cut as "Favorite".

Choose some group or family characteristics that are very distinctive. One layout I plan to do is, "You Know You're a Pedersen When...." Soon after I became engaged to my husband, I found out all Pedersens smell everything, can pick things up with their toes, and can roll their bellies. After both my children were born, I found out this is indeed true. This "legacy" definitely deserves to be scrapped! What "legacies" can your family claim?

Create a scrapbook on "Our Worlds" describing each person's backgrounds, particularly if those backgrounds vary greatly. Include how your upbringings were different and how you come together now. Are you from different parts of town, areas of the country, areas of the world, immigrant cultures, political ideologies or religious backgrounds? How have you benefited from merging cultures?

When you go on a trip, have each person take pictures of the same site. See how the perspectives differ. What did each person notice that the other didn't? You could also do this exercise around your home, group meeting spot or community. Have each person take three to five pictures of favorite things around them, then scrap them. What does

each picture illustrate about the person? How does that contribute to your relationship?

Prompts to trigger journaling

☐ Describe your first impression upon meeting the other person or people.

☐ What is your #1 must-have book?

☐ Who is your favorite character in a book?

☐ What was your most embarrassing moment? Describe it in detail. Then, consider describing embarrassing moments you know about the other person!

☐ Explore how you came to believe your top three values, beliefs or priorities.

☐ What is something you would *never* do, no matter what?

☐ Use five adjectives to describe yourself. Expand on each one.

Now describe the other person/people.

☐ *Aloha* and *mahalo* are the two most important words in the Hawaiian language. What in your opinion are the two greatest words in your life?

☐ What is your ideal summer day together?

☐ What fear have you overcome about your relationship?

☐ What are your pricey or guilty pleasures?

☐ What is a favorite item of clothing from your loved one's closet?

☐ Imagine you are given enough time to pack an adult sized daypack before you evacuate ahead of a storm—what do you pack? *Note:* whatever you don't take is likely to be blown away by the storm.

If both of us were the same, one of us would be unnecessary.
—Unknown

Majestic
by Terri Davenport

Sometimes it takes someone else forcing us to look at circumstances another way before we can realize their significance. "I was annoyed when Mark took this picture," writes Terri. "We were on our way home with a van crammed full of four kids, luggage and Christmas presents... and we were still 45 minutes from home... Mark decides it's the perfect opportunity to pull off the side of a country road to take a picture. Irritating! It was only days later when I saw the picture again that I was able to appreciate it. Mark captured a beautiful picture but the meaning behind the picture is even more important to me." It's a simple layout, just a transparency over a photo enlargement, but for Terri it serves as "a reminder that God is always present in maintaining the beauty and harmony in nature...and in marriage."

Supplies: Cardstock is Stampin' Up. Mini brads are Making Memories. Transparency is Hewlett-Packard. Fonts are Scriptina (downloaded from www.onescrappysite.com); AmerType by Bitstream.

I was annoyed when Mark took this picture. We were on our way home with a van crammed full of four kids, luggage and Christmas presents. The kids were still soaring on the high that only the Christmas season can bring...a unique mixture comprised of too many cookies, running around with their cousins and opening gifts. The weather wasn't terrible, but it was December in Ohio and we were still 45 minutes from home. Instead of sharing my mental view, Mark decides it's the perfect opportunity to pull off the side of a country road to take a picture of the scenery. Irritating! It was only days later...picture again that I was...it. Instead of remember...I consider how fun...running around the e...

Majestic

Everyone is kneaded out of the same dough but not baked in the same oven.

—Yiddish Proverb

It is the mind which creates the world around us, and even though we stand side by side in the same meadow, my eyes will never see what is beheld by yours, my heart will never stir to the emotions with which yours is touched.

—George Gissing

Our Boys
by Lisa Bakowski

For this layout, Lisa and her husband both described what they love about "their boys". She chose a feminine handwriting font for her responses, and a more masculine font for his, and also used different colors of cardstock. Notice how Lisa used round tacks to add interest to the straight lines of this layout.

SUPPLIES: Paper is Chatterbox and A.W. Cute. Cardstock is Bazzill Basics. Fonts are 2Peas Ditzy (downloaded from www.twopeasinabucket.com); butterbrotpapier (downloaded from www.scrapvillage.com); and Stamp Act (downloaded from http://members.aol.com/fontner/). Tacks are Chatterbox. Photo turns are 7Gypsies.

❑ Write about one of your perfect moments.

❑ Complete this thought: The best way to earn my respect is to....

❑ Write about the role of the other person/people in your happiness.

❑ Assume that an investigator wanted to learn more about you, and he only had your wallet or purse. What would the investigator learn about you from those items?

❑ What is your favorite way to wear yourself out?

❑ If you could create a bumper sticker that said "I brake for...", how would you complete it? Why?

❑ What is the best way to "bribe" you into doing something you would not really want to do?

❑ Describe the first time when you felt awe.

❑ What is your favorite comedy one liner? What about it resonates with you?

❑ What three major choices brought you to this point in your life?

❑ Write down how you'd like to see the other person succeed.

❑ A fun prompt: What's your silliest nickname? Write about a time when you had a good laugh about it. List your nicknames for each other.

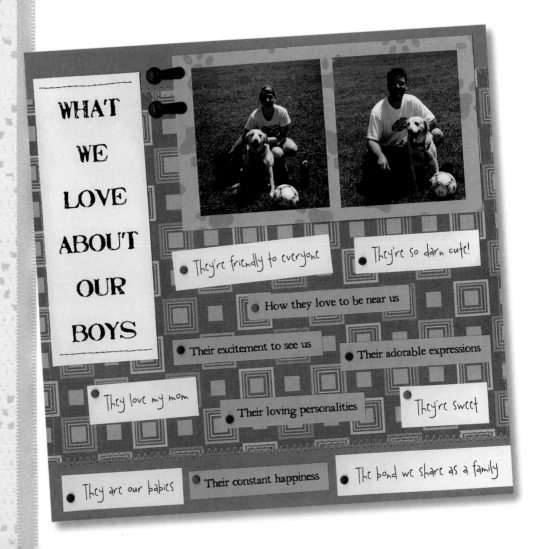

- What are your favorite forms of entertainment? Name your favorite movies, books, music, etc.
- Describe your political ideologies/leanings.
- Compare and contrast your taste in foods.

- What are your favorite ways to relax?
- Describe each person's personality: Introvert/extrovert, laid back/obsessive, etc.

A wonderful realization will be the day you realize that you are unique in all the world. There is nothing that is an accident. You are a special combination for a purpose... Don't ever believe that you have nothing to contribute. The world is an incredible unfulfilled tapestry. And only you can fulfill that tiny space that is yours.

—Leo Buscaglia

Abby & Mom / Mom & Abigail
by Janet Ohlson

The journaling on this layout describes Janet and her six-year-old daughter. It reveals what they like best about each other, each in their own words.

To maintain a look of continuity, the same papers were used on both pages of the layouts... with different results. "My daughter and I each did a page," explains Janet. "Abby really did everything on her page except measuring and cutting the paper. She decided what to use and where to put it, and she even inked the edges herself." Including children's thoughts and opinions on layouts helps them feel like they are contributing to a family project and that what they think matters.

SUPPLIES: Paper, tacks, buttons, stickers and bookcloth are Chatterbox. Cardstock is Bazzill Basics. Ink is Stampin' Up.

We may be blinded by our own perceived flaws, but those who love us have clearer vision.
—Sarah Ban Breathnach

Friends
by Emily Van Natter

Attraction of Opposites
by Jackie Siperko

Both Emily and Jackie used a variety of letter stickers, embellishments and fonts to describe the differences between two people. Notice that, despite their differences, the bottom line of both layouts is the same: their relationship works for them. "Together they couldn't be happier," writes Jackie. NOTE: Emily's layout was inspired by one done by Jennifer Ditz McGuire in *Designing with Words*; be sure to check out this resource for more creative ideas on incorporating words in your layouts.

SUPPLIES (*FRIENDS*): Paper is KI Memories and SEI. Stickers are Foofala, SEI, All My Memories and Making Memories. Stamps are Hero Arts. Ink is Anna Griffin. Alphabet charms and circle tags are Making Memories.

SUPPLIES (*AN ATTRACTION*): Paper is Mustard Moon, 7Gypsies, Daisy D's and Carolee's Creations. Fonts are Heather, Plastique and Ace Bingham. Flower letters are Making Memories. Tag rub on letters are Art Warehouse.

Photos to include

❑ Photos from around your home, meeting spot, community or vacation site, taken by each person

❑ Photo of each person individually

❑ Photos of each of you engaged in favorite activities

❑ Photos from favorite memories

❑ Photo of other person wearing your favorite outfit

Memorabilia to include

❑ Brochures, maps, business cards from vacations ("evidence" of what you each noticed during the trip)

She said... She said...

Tolerance and celebration of individual differences is the fire that fuels lasting love.

—Tom Hannah

The moment one gives close attention to any thing, even a blade of grass it becomes a mysterious, awesome, indescribably magnificent world in itself.

—Henry Miller

There are souls in this world which have the gift of finding joy everywhere and of leaving it behind them when they go.

—Frederick Faber

Perspective

by Marpy Hayse

This moment captured in an antique store became a lesson in perspective. While in the store, Marpy's husband turned to her and said he needed to take a picture, just as she was thinking she wanted to take one.

However, the pictures they took were quite different. She was struck by their difference in perspective, in what was important for each of them to preserve. He saw the scene as a whole, while she was interested in the details. Her journaling comments on how that difference in perspective plays out in their marriage.

You could try a similar exercise with someone close to you—just hand off the camera at some event. See how your pictures differ, both in subject and vantage point, then include your insights in your journaling.

SUPPLIES: Cardstock is Bazzill Basics. Letter stickers are Creative Imaginations and Wordsworth. Photo tiles are Sarah Heidt Photo Craft. Stickers are Creative Imaginations and Nostalgiques for EK Success. Circle tags are Pebbles Inc.

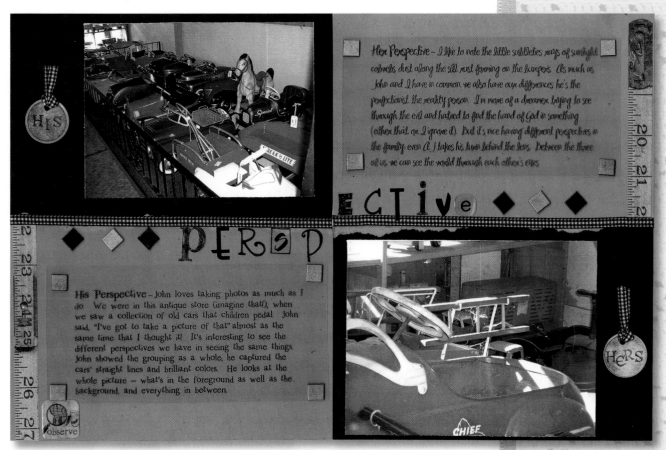

- ❑ Recipes for favorite foods
- ❑ Receipts from "pricey pleasures"
- ❑ Scans of favorite game boards and/or pieces
- ❑ Maps of where you are from
- ❑ Brochures, flyers, or voter registration card from political activities
- ❑ Scans of items from your wallet or purse

The Story So Far
by Jessie Baldwin

Another way to include two people's perspectives on an event is to use envelopes, as Jessie did here. "I asked each of them to tell me about the day they met," explains Jessie. "They each wrote down their story, which I put in the black envelopes. It is cute to read them because, while quite similar, there are the differences in perspective that make them completely great. Their favorite song is "The Story So Far", so I thought it would be appropriate to use that for the title."

SUPPLIES: Paper is 7Gypsies and Paper Adventures. Fonts are Times New Roman and Courier. Stickers and letter rub-ons are Making Memories. Stamps are Hero Arts. String envelopes from www.twopeasinabucket.com. Heart clip is 7Gypsies.

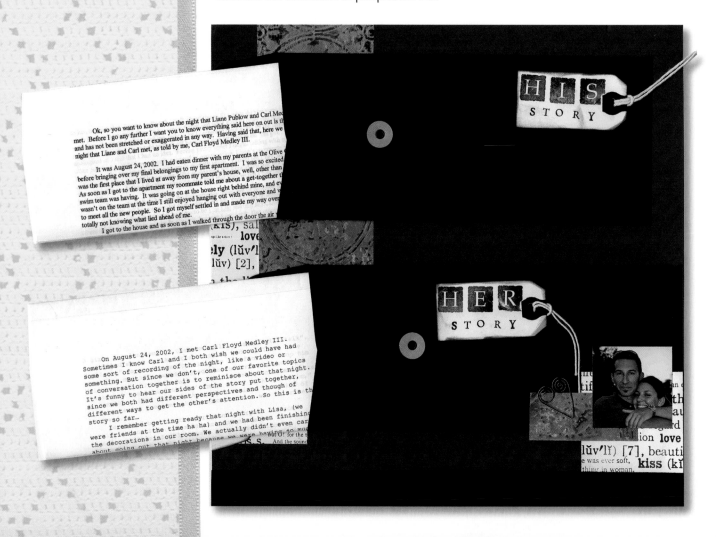

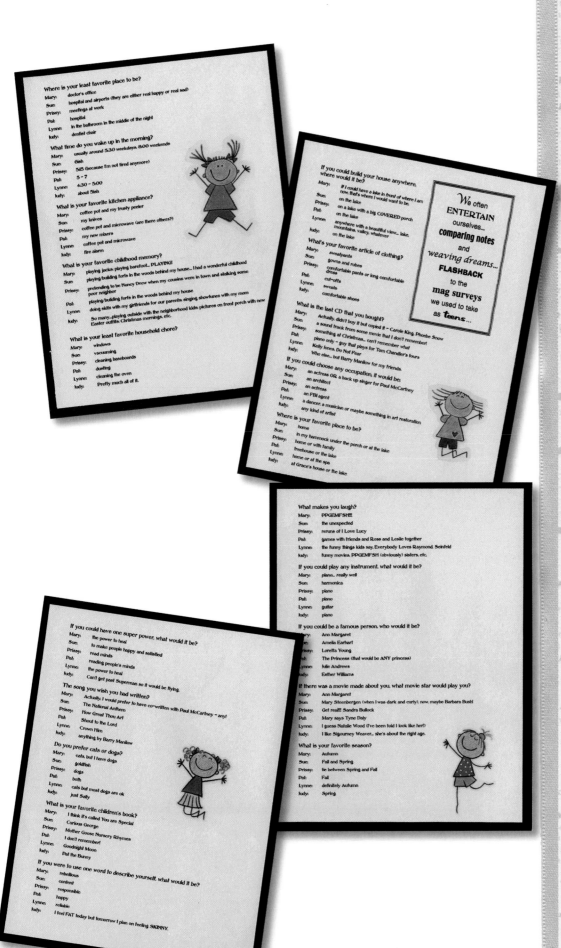

Survey Pages
by Lynne Kariker

Lynne found these questions in one of the "Getting to Know You" questionnaires that travel the Internet. She posed the questions to each of her four friends, and journaled their answers on these layouts. What a neat way to get to know each other better, and illustrate all the different personalities in her group of friends! Simple layouts but packed with content and meaning!

*SUPPLIES: P*aper by DMD. Stickers by Me & My Big Ideas. Fonts are Lucida Calligraphy, Helvetica, Abbess, Techno, Ad Lib BT, Times New Roman and City Scape.

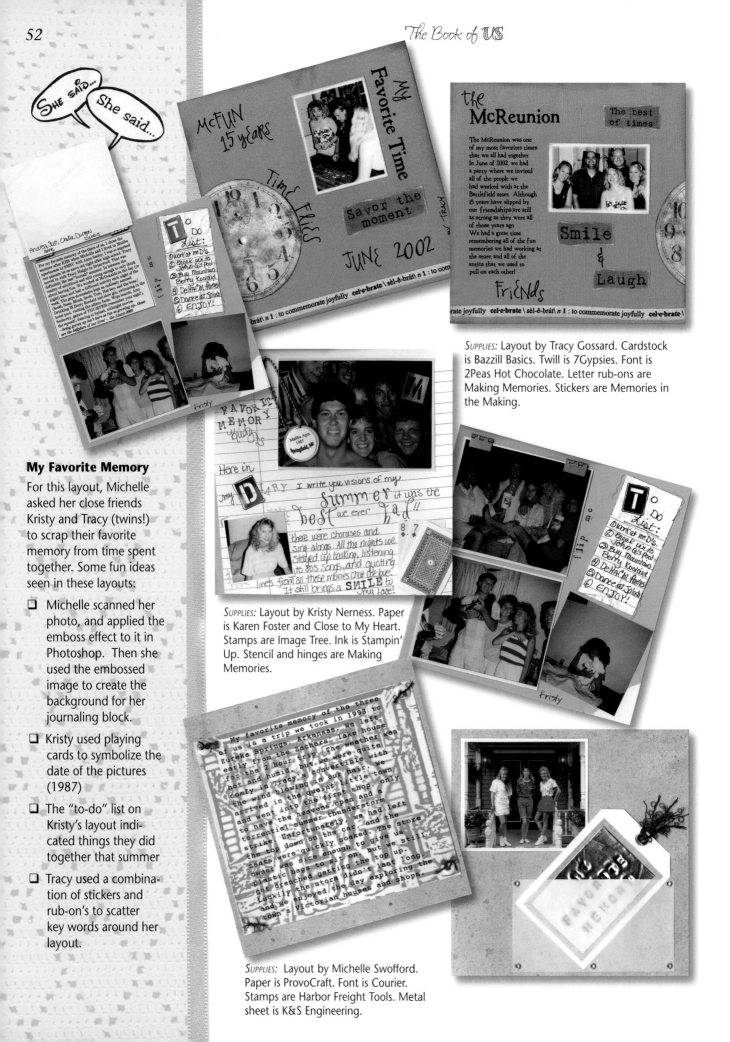

SUPPLIES: Layout by Tracy Gossard. Cardstock is Bazzill Basics. Twill is 7Gypsies. Font is 2Peas Hot Chocolate. Letter rub-ons are Making Memories. Stickers are Memories in the Making.

My Favorite Memory

For this layout, Michelle asked her close friends Kristy and Tracy (twins!) to scrap their favorite memory from time spent together. Some fun ideas seen in these layouts:

❑ Michelle scanned her photo, and applied the emboss effect to it in Photoshop. Then she used the embossed image to create the background for her journaling block.

❑ Kristy used playing cards to symbolize the date of the pictures (1987)

❑ The "to-do" list on Kristy's layout indicated things they did together that summer

❑ Tracy used a combination of stickers and rub-on's to scatter key words around her layout.

SUPPLIES: Layout by Kristy Nerness. Paper is Karen Foster and Close to My Heart. Stamps are Image Tree. Ink is Stampin' Up. Stencil and hinges are Making Memories.

SUPPLIES: Layout by Michelle Swofford. Paper is ProvoCraft. Font is Courier. Stamps are Harbor Freight Tools. Metal sheet is K&S Engineering.

Lee & Shea by Shea Parker

Shea decided to make this album after working for months on their wedding album. As much as she enjoyed the album, she noticed it didn't have any information in it about their everyday lives and who they are as individuals and as a couple. "Lee and I are such polar opposites," she explains. "I think our premarital therapist said it best when she said, 'You need each other to help balance out your extremes.' I don't think either of us will ever get bored, we are always learning from each other and learning to balance things together and in our own lives." She used this album to illustrate how they are different and also noted that they find a common ground in good food. Looking through this album, you see how well-suited they are to each other, despite their differences.

SUPPLIES: Paper is Rusty Pickle and 7Gypsies. Cardstock is Bazzill Basics. Fonts are Calvin & Hobbes, Angelica, Ace Crikey, Crud, CK Cute, 2Peas Tiger Tails, 2Peas Gimme Coffee, Sparkly and SixtySeven Stickers are Li'l Davis Designs. Embellishments are Making Memories.

This Way To

BIRTHDAY CLUB

FRIENDS

Jo Ellen

The glue that holds our group together

Patty

Steady, faithful & true

Do you watch "Miracle on 34th Street" every holiday season, celebrate at the same restaurant or begin every adventure with a special ritual?

This chapter gives ideas for creating a celebrations album around these events.

SUPPLIES: Album is K&Company. Paper and embellishments are SEI. Sparkle paper is Paper Adventures.

Note: Each member has a journaling tag behind it introducing that member. The road trip motif is used throughout the album to signify being part of each other's lives for the long haul.

The hostess with the 'mostest' ~ she really shines at Christmas

Birthday Club
by Sally Ann Finnegan

The original birthday club was formed by six women who were tired of their husbands forgetting their birthdays. Over the course of 13 years, the club has grown to 14 members and the women get together monthly, whether there is a birthday or not. At the December celebration, the following year is planned out as to which member will host or plan each month's event. Sally Finnegan, one of the original members, created this album.

*What I love is near at
hand.*
—Theodore Roethke

*Love the moment,
and the energy of that
moment will spread
beyond all boundaries.*
—Corita Kent

Every day's a kick!
—Oprah Winfrey

This kind of "Us" album highlights the celebrations within your relationship. It may highlight official holidays and parties, impromptu festivities to celebrate an achievement, or simply a beautiful spring afternoon.

For this kind of album, ask yourself, "What do we celebrate together? How do we celebrate together? When have we celebrated together?" Your answers will provide focus and direction, and will form the outline of an album.

When I was working on this chapter, I e-mailed with my friend Wanda about the essential keys to celebrations, tossing around the idea of universal keys to "properly" celebrating holidays and such, as well as those specific to each household. She later commented to me that she really struggled with this question. She e-mailed back, saying that she was stuck in the mode of thinking only of her family from childhood, with her mom and dad "...Engineer grump that he is, he didn't see the point in fireworks. We didn't have a routine for Easter, had limited birthday parties," she confided.

Keys to Our Celebrations Album
by Wanda Thornton

For this project, Wanda used a sarabooks album by Hot Off the Press to describe the "keys" to her family's celebrations. She chose specific holidays, such as birthdays, Fourth of July and Christmas along with ordinary celebrations, such as their morning and nighttime rituals. Then she tied it neatly together on the last page with the "Keys to ALL our celebrations: Family, Friends, Fun." Think of your keys to celebrations and scrap them!

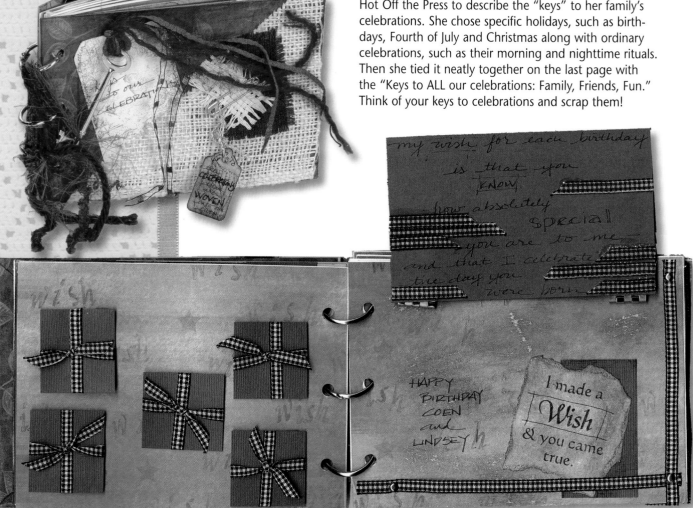

BIRTHDAY CLUB

Supplies (Cover): Paper, key and fibers are Hot Off the Press. Inks are Ranger. Tags are Avery.

Supplies (Birthday): Paper, quote and brads are Hot off the Press. Inks are Ranger. Ribbon is Offray. Hinges are Time To Embellish.

Supplies (Thanksgiving): Paper is Hot Off the Press, Cardstock is Bazzill Basics. Paper is painted with acrylics. Ribbon is Offray and Wrights. Tags are Avery. Twill and staples are Wanda-ful Wonders. Tags were dipped into various acrylic paints that were watered down.

Supplies (Celebrate the Night): Paper is Hot Off the Press. Black tags, screen, aluminum tape, and staples are Wanda-ful Wonders. Metal ornament with black ribbon from an old felt hat. Silver pen by Creative Memories. Calligraphy pen by Zig.

Love is a verb.
—Clare Boothe Luce

I wake at dawn with a winged heart and give thanks for another day of loving.

—Kahlil Gibran

Happiness, in order to be maintained, must be shared.

—Carolyn Warner

Happiness is excitement that has found a settling down place, but there is always a little corner that keeps flapping around.

—E. L. Konigsburg

Life may not be the party we hoped for, but while we are here we might as well dance.

—Unknown

Traditions in Our Relationship
by Erica Shaw

"This is a layout about all of the day to day traditions I find Mike and I do without even thinking about it," explains Erica. "They define our relationship. The little DiBona notebook at the bottom is to add special moments in our relationship as they happen." (*Note*: Erica has appeared in three of my books now, scrapbooking her thoughts and feelings about her boyfriend Mike. I'm happy to report that they got married in August 2004.)

SUPPLIES: Paper is ProvoCraft. Cardstock is Bazzill Textures. Stamp is Stampin' Up. Ink is StazOn and Stampin' Up. Heart and notebook are DiBona Designs. Fonts are Scraps Ahoy Beach Comber and MS Reference. Metal Words are Making Memories. Design inspired by Leslie Lightfoot.

But once she started working on her album, she realized she didn't have to start at the beginning with her family of origin. She could choose to highlight a different "Us". She later revealed she was "thinking the Thornton's were bah humbug... but NOT! It's been such a healing project to work on! I'm more than I thought!"

I think many people might fall into the same trap, limiting their thoughts of "celebrations" to just holidays, or just childhood memories, or whatever. When faced with that "stuck" feeling, Wanda forced herself to look beyond her automatic thoughts, and focus instead on her family today—her husband and two kids.

Almost immediately, she found many reasons why they celebrate together, even daily reasons. She compiled them into her "Keys to Our Celebrations" album (pages 56 to 57), which emphasizes the central theme of togetherness, and each person's role within their family celebrations and traditions. This fits perfectly when you consider the most basic definition of the word celebrate: "To show happiness that something good or special has happened, by doing such things as eating and drinking together or playing music."

Like Wanda, I encourage you to dig deeper in your thinking about celebrations. Seek out those moments that might otherwise go

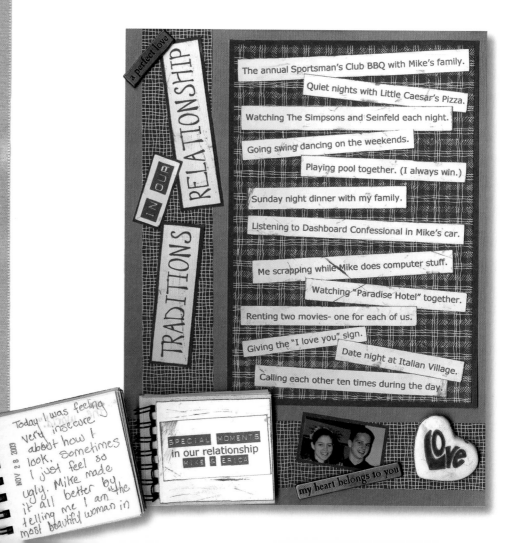

unnoted, and, well, uncelebrated. Brainstorm about the times when something has happened and it all worked out. Think of the times when you breathed a collective sigh of relief. Think of the times when you were each bursting with pride. Think of the times you wouldn't trade for anything in the world. Then scrap them.

Why is this theme important?

As you create pages about this aspect of your relationship, you can't help but remind yourself of all you've celebrated together and all the celebrations yet to come. These are the people to whom you've chosen to commit yourself, the people to whom you dedicate space in your schedule and your heart. Truly, every moment you spend with them can be a form of celebration.

You choose to spend your most joyful moments with them, just as they choose to be with you—be mindful of this intent and document this dedication and affection in your scrapbooks.

In your scrapbook...

Angie Donaldson has provided an excellent template for a generic celebration album, called, "I Loved It When..." (see page 60). You can make it specific by providing examples from your own life. In her example, she included 20 examples of celebrations within her marriage and in the life of her family. She incorporated "big" moments, such as when her husband proposed to her, their wedding and honeymoon, college graduations and the births of their sons.

Celebration Traditions
by Jennifer Newton

Jennifer's journaling documents some of the traditions she enjoyed while growing up, traditions she shares with her family today. Notice that while she straight-cropped her photos, she added visual interest to her layout with her "wonky" journaling box and border. To recreate this layout for your own album, make a list of traditions your family has borrowed from your childhood and include pictures that illustrate those traditions.

Supplies: Vellum and cardstock are National Cardstock.

BIRTHDAY CLUB

Take time to laugh—it is the music of the soul.
—Old English prayer.

Be truly glad! There is wonderful joy ahead.
—1 Peter 1:6

Celebrate the happiness that friends are always giving,
Make every day a holiday and celebrate just living!
—Amanda Bradley

She also included "little" celebrations such as making their sons smile, wrestling and playing with the kids, helping with housework, acting silly and saying "I Love You". You can create a similar album by jotting down ideas on how to complete the statement, "I Loved It When..." Another statement you could consider is "We Were So Proud When..."

For military families, your moments of celebration could reflect the undertone of military life. How are your celebrations different because a loved one serves in the military?

Consider documenting everyday moments that non-military families might not experience. Include layouts of celebrations in the different places you've lived, focusing on the idea that being together makes celebrations more precious.

Document religious celebrations in your home and faith community. How does your faith feed your relationship? What religious aspects have you added to "everyday celebrations"? Include appropriate prayers of thanksgiving and/or religious text.

Dear Dan,

This year we will be celebrating our 18th wedding anniversary. Through many mountain tops and valleys our love has sustained throughout the years. My desire is that this small gift will always remind you of a few things that say......

I Loved It When....

TRUE LOVE

1985

we were

Dating

BIRTHDAY CLUB

Too much of a good thing can be wonderful
—Mae West

I finally figured out the only reason to be alive is to enjoy it.
—Rita Mae Brown

Life itself is the proper binge.
—Julia Child

Always look out for the sunlight the Lord sends into your days.
—Hope Campbell

Find the good—and praise it.
—Alex Haley

Do the best you can in every task, no matter how unimportant it may seem at the time. No one learns more about a problem than the person at the bottom.
—Sandra Day O'Connor

I Loved it When...
by Angie Donaldson

Angie made this album for her husband of 18 years during a difficult time in their lives. She presented it to him on Valentine's Day 1999 with her own ideas and concepts of how she wanted to encourage him. Her husband has been a pastor at one church throughout their marriage. "Being in the ministry brings about many challenges but most of all blessings," explains Angie. "Due to my husband's integrity, perseverance, love and compassion, he has remained faithful to God, the church, but most of all his family." She made this album to show him how happy she is to call him her husband and to show him how proud she is to call him her children's father. Thus, the title "I Loved it When..."

SUPPLIES: Paper is K&Company and Close To My Heart. Cardstock and brads are Bazzill Basics. Vellum is Close To My Heart. Lettering is Making Memories. Cork letters are Creative Imaginations. Ribbon is Offray. Rose paper clip is Nostalgiques. Picture frame is K&Company. Adhesive is Glue Dots.

Anniversary Cruise
by Liz Enos

These layouts are a part of an album that features photos of Liz and her husband on their anniversary vacation. Liz also included some really heartfelt journaling about the evolution of their marital relationship over the years. "One of the best things about a trip like this is that it reminds us how much we have in common," Liz writes, "and how much we enjoy each other's company...On this trip we really broke out of the box and re-connected." It would be easy enough to just scrap these pictures, and let them speak for themselves, but including this kind of journaling helps make the album all the more meaningful.

Create an album of "Everyday Celebrations". What reasons does your "Us" find to celebrate? Include events such as a good grade on a spelling test, a light rush hour, losing a tooth, a job promotion, snuggles in the morning, late night giggles, an e-mail from an old friend, finishing home renovations, getting published, physical triumphs, the first day of spring, and the last day of summer vacation.

Create an Anniversary album that documents how you have celebrated each anniversary in your relationship. Journal about how you spent the day, places you went, what you talked about, and what you were grateful for that year. Use it as a tool to mark time—what was your life like at that point each year? Let it become a testimony to the strength and endurance of your relationship.

Prompts to trigger journaling

❑ What are some traditions in your relationship? How do they factor into your celebrations? What traditions from your childhood would you like to keep?

❑ How do celebrations during your childhood differ from celebrations in your life now? What do you miss from that time? What do you appreciate about today's celebrations? How did your partner's or friend's family celebrate differently?

❑ When have you included other people in your celebrations? Do you do that often?

❑ What have you celebrated with people outside of your family, relationship or group? Think of times with friends, co-workers, social club members, etc.

Supplies: Paper is Chatterbox. Cardstock is Bazzill Basics. Font is 2Peas Hot Chocolate. Stickers are Sharon Soneff and Chatterbox. Punch is Marvy Uchida. Photo corners are Canson. Eyelets by Making Memories.

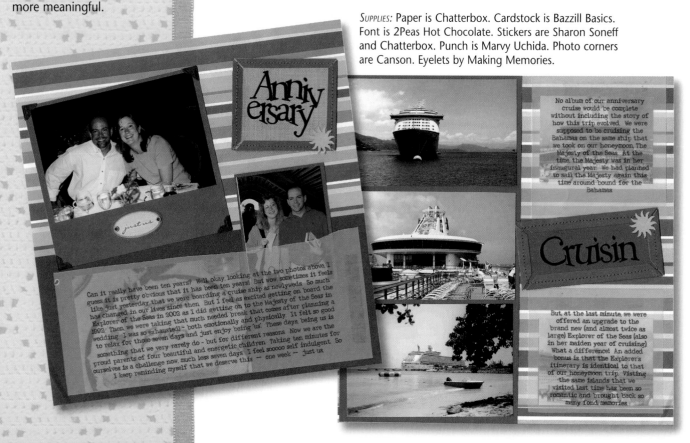

- What are some of the _____ (insert adjective here: funny, weird, heartwarming, romantic, handmade) cards you have received as Valentines?

- What unexpected and/or funny things have happened at birthdays? Do you have pictures? What stories do you recall of other birthdays?

- Write about a road trip that you have taken during the holidays that proved interesting.

- How do "special day" holidays (birthdays, Mother's Day, Father's Day) make each person feel? What habits and traditions encourage the "celebratee" to feel special?

- What are some "keys" to your celebrations? What has to happen every birthday, Easter, Halloween, Memorial Day, etc?

- What rewards do you offer for a job well done or successful completion of a project?

- How does each person prefer to celebrate? According to each person in your "Us", what makes the perfect celebration? Big, boisterous parties? Intimate dinners at home? A week on the lake? Include each person's responses.

- What are some common phrases said in your house during holidays?

- How do you celebrate the last day of school each year? What do you do to prepare for school each year?

- Describe some "success celebrations": job promotions, new jobs, acing a test, getting in the college of choice, mastering a skill, finishing a project, completing a workshop or program, etc.

- Write about a time when you shared a gift with someone else. (Examples: playing together with a new toy as a child, or sharing tea and cookies with

Happy Holle Days
by Holle Wiktorek

"We have a large family with my grandparents, six children, thirteen grandchildren, ten great grandchildren, and two great-great grandchildren," says Holle. "That is too many gifts for my mother to afford, so I suggested she give everyone a scrapbook. Each year I agree to take photos and make the pages for her to color copy and give as gifts... although this gift is inexpensive, the meaning is priceless and preserves our family, and it can be shared within each family household."

SUPPLIES: Cardstock is DMD. Font is Angelina. Letter stickers are Stickopotamus. Stencil is Wordsworth. Beads and sequins are Westrim. Twistel is Making Memories. Wire is Artistic Wire. Scrapsilk is I luv scrapbooking. Adhesive is Therm O Web.

He Takes the Cake & Holiday Quiz

by Pam Canavan

These layouts reveal some celebration traditions in the Canavan family. Every Christmas, Pam and her son create a quiz with holiday trivia. "It is one of our favorite holiday traditions," she writes, "although I don't know how well 'quiz-ees' like it, since they don't ever get them all right!" The other page documents the many birthday cakes her husband has made—cakes are a big part of their celebration. Think of your own family festivities. What elements have become traditions?

a friend as an adult, a trip for both of you.)

❑ What are some of the small but meaningful events in your life? Do you recognize them as just a part of the whole life? What events would you place on a beach scene to represent pieces of sand on the Beach of Life?

❑ Create a page of awards that family members have won. How does that bring you together? Do the awards reveal any common interests or talents?

❑ Consider all the different things you celebrate together, the things you take joy in together. Are the celebrations sweeter because of who you celebrate with? How?

❑ What does your "Us" hope to one day celebrate? What do you look forward to celebrating?

Photos to include

❑ A photo of one of you receiving an award

❑ Photos of birthday parties

❑ Photos taken on each anniversary

❑ Photos depicting a timeline, working towards a goal, then the successful result

❑ Photos of celebration "keys"—cakes or specific recipes, balloons, breakfast in bed, giggles and happy faces, etc.

Memorabilia to include

❑ Award certificates and/or ribbons (or scans of them)

❑ Scans of recipe cards

❑ Ticket stubs or brochures for places visited on celebration trips

❑ Shaker box for sand, dirt, stones, leaves, etc. procured during celebration trips

SUPPLIES (CAKES): Paper is KI Memories. Font is CK Artisan. Brads are Making Memories. Label is Me & My Big Ideas.

SUPPLIES (HOLIDAY QUIZ): Paper is Chatterbox. Font is CK Cute. Foam stamps and paint are Making Memories. Rivets are Chatterbox.

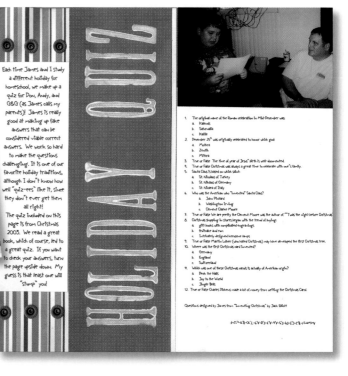

Anniversary Album
by Holle Wiktorek

Holle created this album to celebrate each year of her marriage. She adds one spread to the book each year, describing where they were and how they celebrated. This album reveals a lot, from the tour through scrapbooking trends (paper piecing, pop ups, paper dolls), to Holle's variety of hairstyles (long, short, highlights, blonde, brown). While looking through the album, Holle comments that she realized they had a different address for each almost every year and it shows all the states where they have lived in only a short time.

It's also a testimony to the strength of their relationship, despite so much time spent apart while her husband was deployed. By creating an anniversary album, Holle is reaffirming each year that her marriage is something worth celebrating.

SUPPLIES *(Top):* Paper is Masterpiece Studios. Cardstock is DMD. Font is Lauren Script. Stamps are La Pluma and Stampin Up. Inks are Stampin' Up.

Bottom: Paper is Frances Meyer. Cardstock is DMD. Font is Tangerine. Punch is EK Success.

Above: Paper is Rusty Pickle. Cardstock and vellum is DMD. Font is CK Newsprint. Tag is Li'l Davis. Frame is My Mind's Eye. Stamp is PSX. Diecut is QuickKutz. Brads and eyelets are Creative Impressions. Ribbon is Offray.

The Story of US

passionate friends

Our story is a story of PASSIONATE FRIENDSHIP. Everything we do, say, and feel, is based on that foundation of enduring friendship... over the years.

The Story of Us

How We Met

Our meeting was one of fate. I had been going to KU stadium for nearly a year when I went to a party the first Saturday in 1990. One of my soon-to-be roommates had the idea of a friend's house, and one crazy fun...

in KC the weekend after Finals. He wrote down his name, phone number, and address, telling me to call him about the party, and to bring as many friends as I wanted.

Well, I didn't call.

But, a couple of weeks later, I was at Glenwood Theatre seeing "Die Harder" with Craig Brown, and "scoping" guys before the movie started. I'm thinking, "Yeah, he's cute...yeah, he's cute, yeah, he's HOT!! I know that one! David! Over here!"

David, his friend Matt Prichard, and his cousin Adam Olson came over to chat. I asked David if he'd had that party, and he said, "Yeah! We were waiting for you to call!"

So I apologized, and gave him my KC phone number, telling him to call for the next party. And they went to their seats, with his apparently boasting about getting "a hot girl's"

phone number. (So like him!)

He called me the next night to invite me to Worlds of Fun, but I was busy. He kept trying, though, calling every couple weeks, just to "see what was up." We actually talked quite a while, finding many coincidences: I'd lived in KC since I was 3; he, since 3rd grade. We both worked at Metcalf South mall during the same time period. David was very good friends with Randy Goldstein, who was my schoolmate from Kindergarten to 12th grade! He had other friends at Shawnee Mission East high school, and visited them often. He worked at Godfather's Pizza when my family ate there ALL the time. His house was on the way to Jenny Bryant's; I must have passed him mowing the lawn dozens of times (and thought "whatta stud!", so David says!).

Through it all, we'd never met.

In all our conversations, it was good to

Is love in the air? It's time to bring it into the album! This chapter focuses on romantic relationships. These can be married couples or boyfriend-girlfriend.

SUPPLIES: Album is sarabook by Hot Off the Press. Paper, tags, envelopes and quotes by Hot Off the Press. Transparency is Great White. Cover fonts are MA Sexy (downloaded from www.onescrappysite.com), Walkway Condensed and Carpenter. Inside fonts are Lemon Chicken, Willing Race, John Doe, Adorable, Pablo LET by Letraset, Kathleen, Castellar by Monotype and Dymo. Letter stamps are Debra Beagle's Performance Art Stamps. Photo turns are Making Memories. Brads and library pocket are Boxer Scrapbooks. Buttons are Junkitz. Adhesive strip is Therm O Web.

The Story of Us Album
by Angie Pedersen

When we were dating, I read a book by Harville Hendrix that included the phrase, "passionate friends". This little sarabooks album is my description of our "passionate friendship". Each layout tells about a piece of our friendship, such as the things we love, movies and TV shows we watch and things we dream of doing in the future. In this album, I tried to sum up the key components of our relationship and use them to tell The Story of Us.

The Story of US

One man by himself is nothing. Two people who belong together make a world.

—Hans Margolius.

The entire sum of existence is the magic of being needed by just one person.

—Vi Putnam

To love someone is to see a miracle invisible to others.

—Francois Mauriac

When I mention the topic "Book of US" to people, most of them assume I mean a romantic "Us", so this chapter has been a given since the start. It's also a given because of my own relationship with my husband. I can't think of the word "us" without thinking of him. While we were dating, I read a book by relationship expert Harville Hendrix that included the following quote:

"Marriage is not a static state between two unchanging people. Marriage is a psychological and spiritual journey that beings in the ecstasy of attraction, meanders through a rocky stretch of self-discovery, and culminates in the creation of an intimate, joyful lifelong union… it's about the…practice of becoming passionate friends."

David and I have been "passionate friends" for over 14 years now. And that's just what I want to record in my "Us" scrapbook—the story of how we became passionate friends, what forms our friendship has taken, the evidence of the strength of our relationship and the signs of our love for each other. I want my children to know about love, marriage, compromise, and how to draw strength and comfort from another person. I want it to be a testimony of what the power of love and a committed loving relationship can bring forth.

If you are thinking about making a Book of Us about the romantic relationship in your own life, I encourage you to go beyond the basics of how you met and dated. Dig deeper into the dynamics of your relationship. Consider the actual definition of the word "relationship"—A state of connectedness between

Love Notes Album
by Tonia Youngfellow

Tonia made this mini album for her husband "to let him know how special he is to me". She includes such topics as things they talk about, travel dreams, words to describe him, and date night. She also included a list of song titles that make her think of him or them as a couple. It's obvious from her journaling how much Tonia and her husband enjoy spending time together.

SUPPLIES: Paper is 7Gypsies, Paperbilites, ProvoCraft and Karen Fosters Design. Stickers are Bo Bunny Press, Karen Fosters Design, Me & My BIG Ideas, PSX, Deluxe Designs, Doodlebug and Creative Imaginations. Stamps are All Night Media, Making Memories and Stamp Craft. Ink is Color Box and Paper Craft. Tags are Impress Rubber Stamps. Buttons are Dress It Up. Charms are Blue Moon. Embellishments are Making Memories, Dymo Labeler and Li'l Davis Designs. Fibers are On the Surface. Rub-ons are Craf-T Products. Pens are Zig.

USMC [1989] [1993]

The my guy & military pages could've been combined. Even though you are no longer enlisted, the core values of the Marines are in you. You take great pride in your country & the Marines. I am proud

LIBERTY

troops

groovy kind of love
Phil Collins

This is our song. Remember when we were in K. Falls to announce our engagement. We were outside one day & this song came on the radio. We both loved it and so we decided it was our song. I also loved Crazy For You by Madonna, so that is also our song. The one we danced to at our wedding reception. I love you!

I think of you & ours when these play.

In Your Eyes-
Peter Gabriel

I Swear-
All-4-One

Hero-
Mariah Carey

The Kiss-
The Last of the Mohicans

I Will Always Love You-
Whitney Houston

Nothing Else Matters-
Mettalica

Silent Lucidity-
Queensryche

Love Songs

crazy

for

you
Madonna

MY HERO

true

honest

WONDERFUL

kind

dream

HONOR

STUD

Rico ~ Falling in love with you was the best decision I made. Following the Lord's will to marry you has been such a blessing. You are truly my best friend & I'm glad you're My Guy!

FREEDOM

MY GUY

No. 36R467 2 Cotton Crape...
dresses, stage...
shades such as...
cerise, blue, la...
purposes. Price, per yard......
No. 36R468 Muslin Flags, mount...
Muslin Flags.
Size...6 x9½ inches. Price, per gross...
Size...8 x14 inches. Price, per gross...
Oilcloths.

If you press me to say why I loved him, I can say no more than it was because he was he and I was I.
—Montaigne

Married couples who love each other tell each other a thousand things without talking.
—Chinese Proverb

When you love someone all your saved up wishes start coming out.
—Elizabeth Bowen

Love is friendship set on fire.
—Jeremy Taylor

Love is a sign from the heavens that you are here for a reason.
—J. Ghetto

The most subtle flattery a woman can receive is that conveyed by actions, not by words.
—Susanne Curchod Necked

Sexiness wears thin after a while and beauty fades, but to be married to a man who makes you laugh every day, ah, now that's a real treat!
—Joanne Woodward (married to Paul Newman)

To Our Children
by Irene Mueller

What are your rules for a happy marriage? Think of all the things that you've learned about marriage (from either good or bad examples in your life) and pass those lessons along to children in your life. Include a triple-matted photo and some photo corners, and you're done!

SUPPLIES: Fonts are Baskerville Old Face, Lucida Handwriting and Calligrapher. Stamps are Hero Arts. Eyelets are Doodle-bug. Photo corners are Canson.

people, especially an emotional connection.

Describe your "state of connectedness." How are your lives connected? How do your hearts, minds, and lives mesh? What evidence do you have to show that connection? Give specific examples from your lives, illustrating the bond between you. How would you tell "The Story of Us"?

Ultimately, I think it's a story best told by both people, though I realize that is often an optimistic approach. Try at least asking for the other person's input on pieces of the story. Ask what they would like to see included in the telling of the story.

My friend Libby did a layout on things she loves about her husband. It's a simple but classic layout, incorporating those "little things" that she loves about him. She noted each thing on little strips of paper, "scattered" around a picture of him. What kinds of things does she love? "The fact that he always keeps the gas tank filled for me", "the respect he shows his parents", "the great foot massages that he gives", "his faith in me". (This guy sounds like a real keeper!)

The list she created will also help remind their children of the loving relationship their parents share, enabling them to recognize these signs of love when they see them in their own life. Likewise, I know

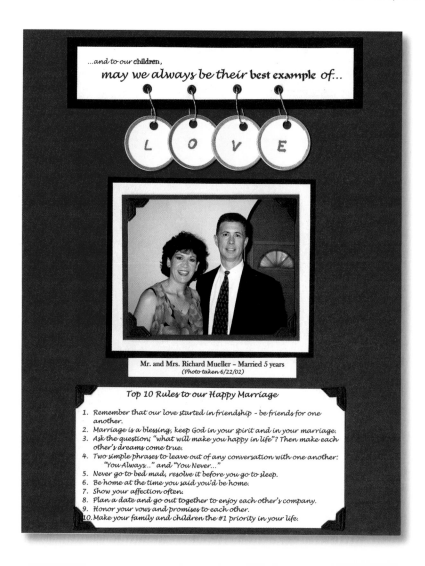

...and to our children, *may we always be their best example of...*

L O V E

Mr. and Mrs. Richard Mueller – Married 5 years
(Photo taken 6/22/02)

Top 10 Rules to our Happy Marriage

1. *Remember that our love started in friendship - be friends for one another.*
2. *Marriage is a blessing; keep God in your spirit and in your marriage.*
3. *Ask the question; "what will make you happy in life"? Then make each other's dreams come true.*
4. *Two simple phrases to leave out of any conversation with one another: "You Always..." and "You Never..."*
5. *Never go to bed mad, resolve it before you go to sleep.*
6. *Be home at the time you said you'd be home.*
7. *Show your affection often.*
8. *Plan a date and go out together to enjoy each other's company.*
9. *Honor your vows and promises to each other.*
10. *Make your family and children the #1 priority in your life.*

that not all of my kids' friends have that kind of relationship example. I want my kids to not only see living examples each day, but have concrete written documentation as well. I can offer them that in a scrapbook.

Why is this theme important?

This theme is important for two reasons:

1) A Book of Us about a romantic relationship reminds you of everything you have faced together and the joys you have shared along the way. Each time you look at this scrapbook, you will smile, remembering why you are together in the first place.

2) A Book of Us about a romantic relationship can provide children with an example of a "real-life" loving relationship. Whether those children are your own, your nieces and nephews, or some other children in your life, providing examples of committed loving adult relationships is critical to helping children achieve that in the future.

Make Me Laugh & Make Me a Better Woman
by Jennifer Newton

These layouts are striking in their simplicity—proof that strong photos paired with meaningful journaling make powerful layouts. The topics are insightful as well. Ask yourself how your significant other makes you a better person. Ask yourself how that person makes you laugh. Then ask how you make them laugh, too! Type your responses into the computer, print it out on cardstock, slap on a matted photo, and you're more than halfway done!

Note: Jennifer made the silver embellishments by pressing a stamp into hot UTEE.

Supplies: Cardstock is National Cardstock. Stamp is Magenta.

...There are a few rules I know to be true about love and marriage: If you don't respect the other person, you're gonna have a lot of trouble. If you don't know how to compromise, you're gonna have a lot of trouble. If you can't talk openly about what goes on between you, you're gonna have a lot of trouble. And if you don't have a common set of values in life, you're gonna have a lot of trouble. Your values must be alike. And the biggest one of those values...your belief in the importance of your marriage.

—Morrie Schwartz

I Love The Way You Make Me Laugh

Brad, you have this amazing ability of making me laugh. I love you for that. You share this amazing world of humor and downright goofiness of a child but still hold me close every night like my strong gallant knight in shining armor. I truly am blessed.

Jennifer - December 2002

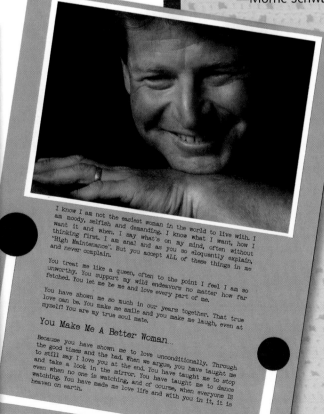

I know I am not the easiest woman in the world to live with. I am moody, selfish and demanding. I know what I want, how I want it and when. I say what's on my mind, often without thinking first. I am anal and as you so eloquently explain, "High Maintenance". But you accept ALL of these things in me and never complain.

You treat me like a queen, often to the point I feel I am so unworthy. You support my wild endeavors no matter how far fetched. You let me be me and love every part of me.

You have shown me so much in our years together. That true love can be. You make me smile and you make me laugh, even at myself! You are my true soul mate.

You Make Me A Better Woman...

Because you have shown me to love unconditionally. Through the good times and the bad. When we argue, you have taught me to still say I love you at the end. You have taught me to stop and take a look in the mirror. You have taught me to dance even when no one is watching, and of course, when everyone IS watching. You have made me love life and with you in it, it is heaven on earth.

It's not what you look at that matters. It's what you see.
—Henry David Thoreau

Personally…I think marriage is a very important thing to do, and you're missing a hell of a lot if you don't try it.
—Morrie Schwartz

I have learned not to worry about love; but to honor its coming with all my heart.
—Alice Walker

3) A Book of Us can help you through the hard times in your relationship. It can bring you together, back to your foundation.

In your scrapbook…

Create a "Signs of Us" album. It could feature symbolic photos like Margie Lundy's examples on page 77, photos that symbolize your relationship with your husband, in addition to (or despite) being parents. Take specific photos that illustrate the idea that this is a Book of US because it shows how you are still a couple, even though you have to work it around being parents. You could also skip the parenting angle and just include photos that symbolize your "state of connectedness"—two toothbrushes, your bathrobes on the same hook, your coffee mugs, your key chains, your rings, your hands together—

Just a Man
by Christie Wildes

Romantic relationships aren't always about roses, hearts and mushy-gushy love notes. Being in a committed relationship also presents unique challenges. Scrapbooking about those challenges isn't usually at the top of a to-do list, but creating those layouts can be a powerful experience. By presenting a realistic portrayal of your love relationship, you provide proof that a strong relationship takes work, but is so worth it in the end.

On this layout, Christie writes, "Although he isn't perfect, he is perfect for me." Recognizing and accepting that lack of perfection is a compelling lesson you can share with others, through your layouts.

Supplies: Paper is Colorworks, K & Co, Deluxe Designs and Rusty Pickle. Cardstock is Bazzill Basics. Large Scrabble letters are Making Memories. Scrabble letters are EK Success. Font is Chatterbox Heber.

Ribbon is Offray. Heart clips, bookplate and paint are Making Memories. Pin is Rebecca Sower Attic Collection. Buttons are Stampin' Up. Love pull charm is Marcella by Kay. File folder is Christie's own design.

anything that signifies that your lives are entwined.

Acknowledge the joy of your relationship by writing 12 reasons to be happy if you've been together 12 months or 12 years, or 24 if you've been together 24 months or 24 years, etc. Or create a gratitude journal of however many happy thoughts for each year you've been together.

Create a "What Makes Us US" album, featuring layouts that describe the unique aspects of your relationship. What defines your relationship? Include layouts on various characteristics of you as a couple, as a whole unit. How you

spend your time? What makes you different from other couples? What are your quirks, habits, routines, likes/dislikes, traditions, hobbies and activities?

Create a mini "Book of Giggles." What makes you both laugh? You could include movies that are guaranteed to make you laugh, or certain comedians or specific memories of shared private jokes.

If you have children, ask them how they know their parents love each other. Include their responses on a layout. Let them take some pictures of you two. Off-center photos could even be fine for this because it's you, through their eyes.

Is He the One?
by Amy Melniczenko

Here's a fun idea – try taking one of those quizzes offered in magazines to find out if your significant other is "The One"! "I always talk about how Paul is my soul mate and that I believe that I was destined to be his wife and him, my husband," writes Amy. "I was intrigued that by answering just 11 questions, you can determine if your partner is 'the one.' I decided to put our relationship to the test." Amy took the quiz and proved that he definitely is "The One"! She made her journaling more meaning-ful by expanding on her answers, providing specific examples from their daily life.

Supplies: Cardstock is Bazzill. Fonts are Ghostwriter and Georgia. Diecuts are Outdoors and More, Inc. Stickers are Creative Imaginations. Rubber stamps are PSX. Ink is ColorBox.

Square

by Jennifer Harrison

What are the key "features" or benefits of your relationship? How would you describe it to others? What provides the foundation for your relationship? In this layout, Jennifer describes her marriage like this: "Love is where it begins and ends for us. We're nerds and we're square. We are equals and partners. We're companions and friends, but most of all... we're in love."

SUPPLIES: Paper is KI Memories and Kangaroo & Joey. Cardstock is Bazzill Basics and Pebbles in My Pocket. Stamps are Making Memories and Magenta. Ink is Stampin' Up. Font is Serifa TH BT.

Compile a "Our Book of Gifts", which you could take either of two ways. What gifts do you share with each other? How do your strengths and weaknesses balance each other? Or you could record different material gifts that have been given at various points in your relationship, either for special moments or just because.

Prompts to trigger journaling

❏ Describe the perfect romantic evening or date.

❏ Make a list of the top 10 values or beliefs you have together.

❏ My definition of intimacy is...

❏ What have you learned from each other?

❏ What does your partner bring out in you?

❏ Create a page incorporating a quote from a loved one, translated in various languages. (Try using altavista.com's Babelfish program to translate into other languages).

❏ What have been some of the thunderstorms of your life? Those things that have been loud and troublesome but brought needed water. Create a page of a meaningful storm in your life.

❏ Describe the other person's beauty (inside and out).

❏ List nice things you have done for each other.

❏ When did you each first realize you were in love? How could you tell?

❏ Imagine and describe your perfect weekend getaway together. Assume that you have plenty of time, money and all the planning works. Include all that your senses might experience.

- Describe the other person's hugs.

- What are your five rules for living happily ever after?

- What makes you laugh when you're together? What role does laughter play in your relationship? Do you laugh and play together more or less than other couples you know? What evidence do you have for that assessment?

- How does the word "dedication" apply to your relationship?

- How does the other person allow the fullness of who you are to be expressed?

- Fill in the blank and answer. How I came to love ....

- Write out your personal definition of what love is. Be detailed: a one-line definition may not capture all of your thoughts. Include a definition from both of you.

- Who are your "love mentors"? Who has provided strong examples for a respectful, committed, loving relationship? Do you both look to the same mentors, or do you each have examples from your own personal histories?

- If you could tell the story of your relationship by taking someone to five places, where would you take them?

- How do you communicate your love for another?

- What token do you have that lets you know someone you love is going to stick by you no matter what? What non-traditional tokens of commitment do you have?

Sweetheart
by Emily Van Natter

There's so much going on in this layout! Emily included quotes, song lyrics, a fortune, photos of her and her sweetheart and romantic images she found on the Internet. She strung ribbon across it to help hold in some of the memorabilia. The ribbon could also hold in love notes or messages you've written to each other, describing what makes you each other's sweethearts.

Supplies: Paper is 7Gypsies. Stickers are Susan Branch, Making Memories, Rebecca Sower, Renae Lindgren and Pebbles in My Pocket. Diecuts are KI Memories. Stamps are Ann-ticipations and Hero Arts. Ribbon is Making Memories and Offray. Word definitions are Foofala.

❑ What habits have you created together? What routines have sprung up naturally?

❑ What interests have you developed together in the course of your relationship? Make a list of things you love to do together.

❑ Describe some private jokes you share.

❑ Watch a movie you both love, and then each write what you love most about it. Write about the first time you saw it together. What are your favorite lines from the movie?

Photos to include

❑ Pictures of your first date

❑ Pictures from your wedding

❑ Pictures of each of you individually

Portrait of a Mom & Dad
by Erin Bradley-Hindman

These layouts would fit into a "Signs of Us" kind of album. Look around your home for symbolic scenes, perhaps something that shows that even though you're parents, you are still a couple. For Margie's "Romance" layout, "the lighting quality was actually pretty poor, so I turned it black and white and then colorized it slightly red," she says. "The result was funny since it was a 'pretty' photo of a funny situation." In addition to taking specific photos, you could also look through your stash for indications of your dual roles as parent, and part of a couple, or just examples of your "couplehood", without the emphasis on parenthood.

SUPPLIES: Paper is ProvoCraft, Carolees Creations and Anna Griffin. Font is American Typewriter. Stickers are Nostalgiques. Stamps are Ma Vinci. Transparency by Magic Scraps. Photo turns and brads are Making Memories. Ink is Staz-On. Diamond glaze by Judikins.

- Pictures of you hugging
- A photo of you from behind, with your arms around each other's shoulders or holding hands
- Pictures of "signs of Us"
- Pictures of things that make you laugh

Memorabilia to include

- Receipts from first dates (or scans of them)
- Menus from your favorite restaurants
- Cards included with flower deliveries
- Love notes (or scans of them)
- Doodling featuring the other person's name
- "Signs of love"—receipt from keeping the gas tank full, transcript of voice/e-mails, pressed flowers, etc.

I would rather have one breath of her hair, one kiss of her mouth, one touch of her hand, than an eternity without it.
—"City of Angels"

The greatest thing you'll ever learn is just to love and be loved in return.
—"Moulin Rouge"

Put on your *Dancing* Shoes

We don't go out dancing, like I hear some do, but I do enjoy the occasional pass each other in the hallway, hug, and slow dance move. Of course that usually ends in a big ME TOO from Josh who wants to do the Twist as fast as possible. While the appeal of the slow dance is lost on him, I love it even if it's squeezed in between life and the Twist.

Private *Time*   Just the ~~two~~ of us three

Rememer the days, way back then, when we used to snuggle? At least I think we did. It's hard to remember with all the bouncing, tackling, and tickling. We always exchange those half smiles that say "I love you and if I weren't encouraging my son to jump on you I'd be kissing you honey."

Whoever said *Romance* is dead...   surely had a 4-year-old.

Sometimes I miss our alone time, but I wouldn't trade our not alone time for anything!

Dancing Shoes, Private Time & Romance
by Margie Lundy

(See caption on opposite page.)

SUPPLIES: Fonts are Kunstler Script and Garamond. Digital layouts created using Adobe Photoshop.

Nanny & Poppy Album
by Steph Stanley

You don't have to limit your-self to scrapbooking about your own love relationships —consider documenting those who have served as your "relationship mentors" as well. "I am *so* blessed to have been raised around my great-grandparents," says Stephanie. "I started the book so I have a way to re-member the stories and such so my kids will never forget. I add stuff as I remember it and add pictures as they find them. It's become a kind of relationship journal for me!"

On your layouts, describe how spending time with other couples has affected and enhanced your perspec-tive on loving relationships. What have you learned about what you want from observing others' relation-ships?

SUPPLIES: Paper is K&Company and Stampin' Up.

Love of My Life
by Nicola Clarke

Nicola's journaling begins, "I have always loved a good love story, what girl doesn't?" Take some ideas from this layout, and tell your own love story. Nicola gives some great examples of what to do with lots of different pattern papers, while still leaving room for journaling (hint: it's hidden in a little book attached with the 7Gypsies band at the bottom left of the border).

SUPPLIES: Paper is Chatterbox, 7Gypsies, Carolee's Creations, Doodlebug and Sassafrass Lass. Cardstock is Bazzill Basics. Fabric is Creative Imaginations. Transparency is Daisy

OTHER SUPPLIES: Ribbon, staples and metal photo corner are Making Memories. Foam stamp and elastic band are 7Gypsies. Bottle cap is Li'l Davis. Twist ties are Pebbles Inc. Buttons are Junkitz. Bookplate is Art Warehouse. "V" index card and black stencils are Autumn Leaves. "Life" T-pin by EK Success. Red letters are Foofala. Charms are www.twopeasinabucket.com.

carefree, funny
Peter ... very devoted to us ...

To the outside world we all grow old but not
to brothers and sisters. We know each other
as we always were. We share private family
jokes. We remember family feuds and
secrets, the family griefs and joys.
We live outside the touch of time

Emotional
Caring
Affectionate
Courage
BEAUTIFUL
Sassy
Determined
KIND HEARTED
multiple stupidisms

Princess
Deanie
DRIVEN
Hugs

Golden Child

A brother or sister is a gift to the heart, a friend to
the spirit, a golden thread to the meaning of life.

We know one another's faults, virtues, catastrophes, mortifications, triumphs, rivalries, desires, and how long we can each hang by our hands to a bar. We have been banded together under pack codes and tribal laws.

Having a sibling is like having a best friend you can't get rid of. You know whatever you do, they'll still be there.

The family ties that bind us contain interesting stories to scrapbook. These Book of Us layouts can be about an entire family, a parent and a child, siblings or relatives.

Supplies: Paper is Chatterbox. Cardstock is Bazzill Basics and DMD. Fonts is RW Writing. Stickers are Making Memories and Stickopotomus. Inks are Stampin' Up. Ribbon is Offray. Mesh is Marayuma. Tag, word ribbon, brads and photo turns are Making Memories. Thread labels are Me & My BIG Ideas.

Nicole is the Queen, the backbone of the family. The one that keeps us all together no matter where we are. She is the family orientated one. She is very protective of us and will not let anything come between us. She is the caregiver. She is the one that talk. She is easy to talk to because she doesn't let her emotions stand in the way of the problem. She will tell you straight up if she just a problem. All it takes is an I'm sorry, and it's as if there was never a problem. She will do anything for us. She is a very giving of her time. She is the artsy one. She is the geeky one. She loves forever.

Siblings Accordion Mini Book *by Nicole White*

The album is decorated on the front and back of the accordion, with two pages for each sibling. Each photo hides a journaling tag behind it. Nicole also included family pictures of the five of them, in between each sibling, with hidden photos under the top one. To create this album, she called all of her siblings and asked each one to write a sentence or two on how they feel about the other. "It was very insightful and felt very nice to be able to hear those words from them," said Nicole.

With our genetics, you can't expect anything normal.
— James Pedersen

Remember, as far as anyone knows, we're a nice normal family.
— Homer Simpson

To love and be loved is the greatest happiness of existence.
— Sydney Smith

Never forget that the most powerful force on earth is love.
— Nelson Rockefeller

The best things you can give children, next to good habits, are good memories.
— Sydney J. Harris

Daddy
by Jennifer Newton

Jennifer's "keyword journaling" captures the various roles her husband fills for their children. The photo illustrates those roles perfectly – what a good sport he is for posing for that picture! What photos can you take to help illustrate the roles people fill in your family?

SUPPLIES: Paper is National Cardstock. Fonts are Mom's Typewriter and Vintage Typewriter.

It always makes me chuckle, knowing just how "normal" my own family is. The idea pairs very nicely with a quote from my son, "With our genetics, you can't expect anything normal." Maybe you can't expect "normal" at your house either, but you can use a scrapbook to describe what life is like at your house.

In a family-based Book of Us, try to answer the question, "What is it like to be a member of my family?" Use your layouts to try to paint a picture of what being a member of your family is like. You can do this by listing activities you do together, describing the personalities of each family member, talking about common interests, and using photographs to show genetic similarities. Let your scrapbook pages show what makes your family different from other families.

You can also include pages on relationships between specific family members. How is your relationship with your sister special? What do you enjoy about your relationship with your children? What makes your brother the world's best uncle or your sister the world's best aunt? How did you know your husband would make a good dad? Incorporating answers to these types of questions will provide meaningful journaling for your layouts. Your scrapbooks will become more than just a record of events and activities. Describing "how" and "why" gives solid proof of the relationships you already know exist.

We decorate our Christmas tree the first weekend of December every year. We love going through the ornaments and remembering when we got each one. On Christmas Eve, we leave out cookies & egg nog for Santa. In exchange, Santa leaves snowy footprints.

Christmas Eve

Read Books

We love to read books together! David or Angie read to James & Joanne before bed every night— Harry Potter, the Bible, the Chronicles of Narnia, Caps for Sale, Eloise, The Giggler Treatment, & many more favorites.

Cozies

"Will you cozy me?" James turned the word "cozy" into a verb when he was very young. We love to cozy on the couch, in David's chair - it's a great way to enjoy movies or our favorite TV shows together.

Comfort

If you can give your son or daughter only one gift, let it be enthusiasm.
—Bruce Barton

Children are the anchors that hold a mother to life.
—Sophocles

With boys, you always know where you stand. Right in the path of a hurricane.
—Erma Bombeck

Our Book of Fun
by Angie Pedersen

I created this tag book to show some of the fun things we enjoy doing as a family. I thought about our days and drew out the little moments that make up our time together, like reading books and waking up slowly together in the morning. I also plan to do pages about music we listen to, shows we watch on TV together and Family Game Night. This book provides me with a great excuse to take photos of those everyday kind of moments.

SUPPLIES: Paper and cardstock are Paper Adventures. Tag die by Ellison. Letter stickers are Paper Loft. Letter stamps are Debra Beagle's Performance Art Stamps. Inks by Plaid and Ranger. Photo paper by Epson.

Family Stories Album
by Kathie Rinehart

"Out of all of my scrapbook albums, this is by far my favorite," says Kathie. "I scrapbook so that we will have memories of our lives and this scrapbook above all others is about memories—stories that are pieces of us that I don't want to be forgotten." The journaling on each page is the emphasis; not every event has photos. Kathie suggests keeping a notebook to jot things down as you think of them. Pull from the notebook when you want to add to your family stories album.

Why is this theme important?

This theme is important because family forms the most basic of links; it is the first connection we have at birth. We are instantly connected to our parents and our siblings, as well as our extended families of grandparents, aunts, uncles and cousins. They provide our closest support systems—our own "in-house" cheerleading squads. Scrapbooking about relationships with family members encourages you to remember the joy available to you in your own home, as well as reminding your family members what they mean to you.

In your scrapbook...

Create an "Our Book of Fun." How do you relax and have fun together as a family? List hobbies and activities you enjoy when you spend time together. Think of general themes of topics, such as listening to music and family game night, then include specific anecdotes related to those themes.

Follow Kathie Rinehart's example below and collect various family stories in an album. Think of the stories that come out at every holiday dinner or family reunion. Document the history of the stories, describe all the "characters" involved, include sensory details and plot it all out. Tell the stories so non-family members can understand their significance.

Create a page of the "found" items on a desk or in a junk drawer, such as old receipts, movie tickets, gum wrappers, playing cards, etc. Journal about how these scraps entered your life or how they illustrate the life of your family.

Create a "Signs of Us" layout, describing "signs" for each member of your family. What "marks"

Computer tip: Kathie made "Family Prayer" using her wide-format printer. "I have a blank set up in MS-Publisher that is a custom sized page of 12x12. It makes layouts like this quick and easy and enables me to just concentrate on capturing the memory." (This would also work in MS-Word or MS-Works.)

Supplies: Cardstock is Bazzill Basics. Fonts are Stamp Act, Antique Type, Cloister Black BT and Rockford. Frame is K&Co.

are left in your world? Consider "artwork" left on walls, juice cups left around the house, backpacks in the foyer and sheet music in the kitchen. What are the "signs" that your spouse/son/daughter/you live in your house?

Document your Family Values. What do honesty, trustworthiness, courage, strength, loyalty, patience, determination, compassion, honor, etc mean in your family? Where have you seen examples of the above in your family? Describe specific instances.

Create a basic family tree or a "Cast of Characters" for your current family albums. Define the familial relationships between the people featured in the album, starting with the oldest person and ending with the youngest. Consider noting family similarities, whether genetic characteristics, or hobbies, aptitudes or interests.

Honor family friends or people who are just like one of the family. Journal about influential people who spend a lot of time with your family.

Are you a godparent or religious sponsor? Do you have a godparent or religious sponsor? If so, include the godparent relationship in your scrapbooks. Why is it important to you to be that person's godparent/child? You could ask the other person what your relationship means to them, and include their words. Some album topics could

Crazy Days & This Relationship
by Annie Wheatcraft

These layouts so beautifully capture the essence of the relationship between these siblings. The candid photos reveal their interactions, and Annie's journaling includes insights into their daily life together. She has documented snippets of everyday conversations, what they fight about, how they share, and how they enjoy "a bond that grows over time". Watch the interactions between family members in your own life, and ask yourself how you can capture the essence of their relationship on a layout.

Supplies: Paper is Magenta. Fonts are CK Stenography and Times New Roman. Buckle and ribbon are Making Memories. Ink is Stampendous.

He Loves Me
by Jenn Brookover

"Less then two years apart in age, Jake and Cody have formed quite a bond," says Jenn. "Since Cody was born, Jake has always kept an eye on him and let me know when he needed something. They love to play together and will race trucks and throw balls forever. If Jake goes out the door, Cody is right behind him. If Jake is eating, Cody wants what he is having. Lately though, Cody has become a little possessive of his (and other people's) things. This has caused more than a few outbursts. I know this will pass, I just hope when it does, we end up with more love!"

be "Day Trips with Our Godchildren", "Things We've Learned from Each Other", "What It Means to be a Godparent/child", or just things you enjoy doing together.

Prompts to trigger journaling

❑ How would you capture the cute and adorable about a child in your life?

❑ What has been the messiest event in your life? Maybe making mud pies, cooking with the grandkids or painting a new room?

❑ What makes a good mother/father/sister/brother/aunt/uncle/grandparent?

❑ What are words you want your baby to hear each day?

❑ Describe your family's morning routine.

❑ What do you look for to tell if someone loves you? How do you show others you love them?

❑ How does your family practice/experience religion?

❑ What sounds do you associate with your grandfather? Create a page that "sounds" like him, or events you associate with him. (Could be the hum of the tractor, or snoring, or heavy work boots clumping down the wooden hall floor)

❑ Describe how who you are is a result of efforts by others.

❑ Create an image of what you would like to have together in one year. What are your goals as a couple or family? Think about monetary, possessions, emotional, spiritual, etc.

SUPPLIES: Paper by Paper Adventures. Title font is Black Jack by Typadelic.com. Journaling font is P22 Typewriter. Stamps are Hero Arts (script) and Ma Vinci's Reliquary (stencils). Ink is Vivid. Metal plaque, letters, ribbon and safety pins are Making Memories. Paint is Americana. Tile letters are Westrim Crafts. Transparency is Apollo.

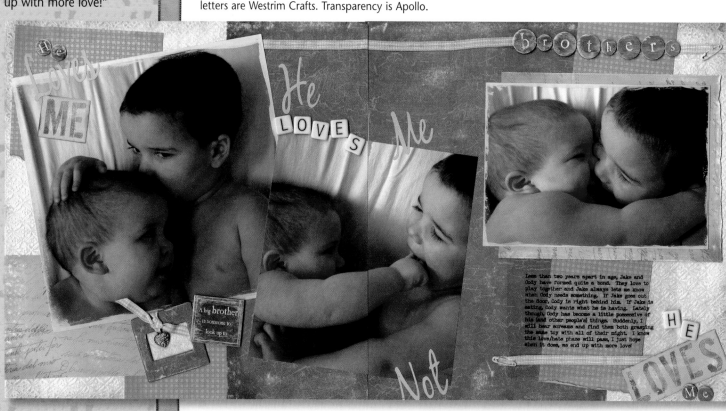

❑ What business cards or other name cards do you have for family members? Create a card page to showcase the different cards. Maybe you have many of your own. Create a page of the history of your business cards.

❑ Using a map of the world, where have your family members come from, and/or where do they live now?

❑ Write of a time when you learned life was not fair to someone you loved. How did you respond?

❑ What are those things you love about your mom? What do you like least?

❑ What are some of the traits you love most about your dad? What are those things you like least about your dad?

❑ Make a list of the top 10 values or beliefs you hold as a family or couple.

❑ What music do you listen to together?

❑ Write about someone who has made a difference in your life. How have you changed as a result of that person's involvement in your life?

❑ How did you occupy time as a child while driving with your parents? What do your children do during road trips now?

❑ What has been your favorite year? What made it so?

❑ Write about the role relaxation has in your life. What do you do to relax together?

❑ What is the cutest thing you have ever heard a child say? Include the dialogue.

A happy family is but an earlier heaven.
—John Bowring

Of all nature's gifts to the human race, what is sweeter to a man than his children?
—Cicero

The laughter of girls is, and ever was, among the most delightful sounds of the earth.
—DeQuincey

My father was often angry when I was most like him.
—Lillian Hellman

Just Like You
by Linda Albrecht

These candid photos really capture the essence of the relationship between these siblings. "I love the moments that I captured between my sons," says Linda. "We always tell our older children that they are an important part of Cort's life and they need to remember to set good examples for him." Linda's journaling reflects that family value. Think about how you can capture the examples your older children set for your younger children or how you and your siblings have set examples for each other, in the past and today.

SUPPLIES: Paper is Chatterbox, Rusty Pickle, ProvoCraft and K&Co. Font is Fulton Art Stamp. Letter stickers Deluxe Design.

There wouldn't be half as much fun in the world if it weren't for children and men, and there ain't a mite of difference between them under the skins.
—Ellen Glasgow

My 10-year-old daughter is my #1 power source.
—Hanan Mikhail Ashrawi

A Lot Like Dad
Coutrney Walsh

As kids, often the last thing we want to do is turn out like our parents. Now grown up with children of her own, Courtney has realized some of her best traits have come from her parents. Courtney wanted to create this layout "because there are so many traits that I know I've adopted from him...some good and some not so good.

Supplies: Paper is Chatterbox. Cardstock is Bazzill Basics. Font is Copperplate. Stamp is PSX. Index tab is Autumn Leaves. Mesh is Magic Mesh. Hinges are Making Memories.

❑ What had you laughing together recently?

❑ Write about the most recent time when someone has done a good deed for you. Keep track of the small kindnesses people in your family do for each other and use them in a layout.

❑ Which person are you grateful for having in your life this year? Write about a time you spent with that person.

❑ What traits did you learn or inherit from your mother? What traits do you think your children have learned or inherited from you? Identify the common traits.

❑ Document the "Rules of the House", addressing things like curfew, housework, TV, food, homework, etc.

❑ Write about a time when you realized how important encouragement from others was to you.

❑ Create a page of fun or funny things that happen at Grandmother's house.

❑ What are some things people in your family always say? Phrases, mispronunciations, etc.

❑ Describe genetic similarities within your family: physical features, aptitudes, interests. Create a page of pictures of family members who look like each other. Maybe list the qualities they share.

❑ What spiritual activities does your family do together? Why do you think that's important?

❑ Describe the balance between strengths and weaknesses of each family member.

Photos to include

☐ Photos that reveal genetic similarities among family members

☐ Photos of your family home

☐ Photos of the whole family together

☐ Photos of the family engaged in a spiritual activity

☐ Photos of "signs" for each family member

☐ Photos of family heirlooms, or significant possessions (furniture, dishes, quilts, etc)

Memorabilia to include

☐ Scans of children's artwork, particularly a drawing of the whole family, or the family home

☐ Notes, cards, and/or e-mails between siblings (or scans of them)

☐ Favorite family recipes

☐ Phone bill depicting calls to family members

☐ Business cards from family members

☐ Screen shot or log of instant message or chat sessions between family members

My Dad
by Amy L. Barrett-Arthur

What a great "moment" to capture! Amy made it more meaningful by adding journaling about what her son likes to do with his dad, and his reaction each day when Dad gets home from work. Notice how she placed her journaling on transparency vertically along the side of the layout for added interest.

SUPPLIES: Paper is K&Company. Cardstock is Bazzill Basics. Font is CK Typeset. Letter stickers are Pebbles. Frame, tags and letter stamps are Making Memories. Ink is Ranger Industries. Pain is Delta. Brads are American Tag and Fastener.

The real menace in dealing with a five-year-old is that in no time at all you begin to sound like a five-year-old.
—Jean Kerr

I'm going to clean up this dump – just as soon as the kids are grown.
—Erma Bombeck

It's not what's on the table that matters, it's who's in the chairs!
—Unknown

If God is love, it makes perfect sense that you are my Godchild.
—Jenna Robertson

There are many ways to measure success; not the least of which is the way your child describes you when talking to a friend.
—Unknown

Grandma always made you feel that she had been waiting to see just you all day and now the day was complete.
—Marcy DeMaree

Happiness is having a large, loving, caring, close-knit family in another city.
—George Burns

Wait for Me & Letters from Mom & Dad
by Amy Farnsworth

Often what one family member does affects the whole family. "The day my brother left on his mission was a hard day for the whole family," writes Amy. She created these layouts to preserve moments of that day. The "Wait for Me" layout captures a moment between her brother and their littlest sister. While pushing her head down with his hand, he told her "not to grow any" while he was gone. The envelopes on the second layout hold letters from her parents to her brother, given the day he left for Spain for two years.

Memories of Love
by Danielle Toews

Danielle's journaling captures the memories of many sensory details, such as the taste of oatmeal cookie dough, the smell of cinnamon and nutmeg and getting tucked into bed with "a million teddy bears". She also includes her feelings about her grandmother's aging. What sensory memories do you have of family members that should be documented in a scrapbook? What will you miss when they're gone? What do you want others to know about your relationship with specific family members?

SUPPLIES: Paper is KI Memories, Chatterbox and 2Busy-Moms. Cardstock is Bazzill Basics. Ink is Colorbox. Pens are Marvy Uchida. Rub-ons are Making Memories.

SUPPLIES: Paper is Pebbles, 7Gypsies and Rusty Pickle. Stamps, paints, bookplates, washer word and mini brad are Making Memories. Ink is Memories and 7Gypsies. Envelope template is Deluxe Designs. Letter stickers are Doodlebug.

SUPPLIES: Paper is 7Gypsies. Stickers are Doodlebug Design (me) and Rebecca Sower (for) and measuring tape stickers. Rub-on alphabet, brads, paper flowers, definition sticker and fabric are Making Memories.

cherish (cher´ish) 1. to hold dear 2. to treasure, adore, value and love 2. to keep deeply in mind

More Than Siblings
by Lindsay Teague

Think of all the things that make a relationship "more than siblings", and document them about your own life. Lindsay created this layout about her best friend and her brother. "They are unbelievably close, and I love to hang out with them," she says. "I thought this poem fit perfectly into their relationship." Notice all the inking, stitching, and metal accents Lindsay added to her layout to add interest, without distracting from the photo.

Supplies: Paper is Melissa Frances. Stickers are Making Memories and Li'l Davis. Canvas letters are Li'l Davis. Stamp is PSX. Ink is 7Gypsies. Ribbons, T pin, snap and safety pin are Making Memories. Ribbon is Offray.

I'm Sorry
by Jennifer Newton

Jennifer's journaling will hit home for many of us. She spends the majority of her time working for "someday", and regrets the time away from her children. "I apologize now and hope all of the time I have invested will someday turn into an opportunity to do all of those things I wish so dearly for now," she writes. "All of my work has a goal; to be with you from the moment you come home from school until the time you go to bed." She promises that the day is "coming". How often do we think these very things, yet leave them unsaid? Use your scrapbook to record them.

Supplies: Cardstock is National Cardstock.

The fact is, there is no foundation, no secure ground, upon which people may stand today if it isn't the family…If you don't have the support and love and caring and concern you get from a family, you don't have much at all. Love is so supremely important. As the great poet Auden said, 'Love each other or perish.'

—Morrie Schwartz, in Conversations with Morrie by Mitch Ablom.

She discovered with great delight that one does not love one's children just because they are one's children but because of the friendship formed while raising them.
—Gabriel Garcia Marquez

There are so many things about my childhood I cannot recall; but of my grandma's house, it seems that I remember all.
—Jessie Wilmore Murton

Traits
by Dana Swords

Dana sliced up close-up photos of each member of her family to illustrate common features. "I always thought my daughter looked like me as a child," says Dana. "When I cut our photos apart and played with them, I found that she has exactly the same facial features as my husband! This was really fun to play with." Dana cut their faces into strips and a second set into quarters. Then she mixed and matched the pieces to create the layout.

Supplies: Paper by Magenta. Stickers are Shotz. Fonts are Modern 20 and Tempus Sans. Snaps are Making Memories.

The Choice
by Pam Canavan

Many decisions a family makes have life-altering results. Scrapbooking the decision-making process may help others make similar decisions. Pam's journaling details the path her family took in deciding to homeschool their son. She describes the circumstances leading up to the decision, the pro's and con's they discussed, their concerns, and the final results. All of those details help paint the picture of this time in their lives.

Supplies: Stickers by Doodlebug. Font is Garamond. Embellishments are KI Memories.

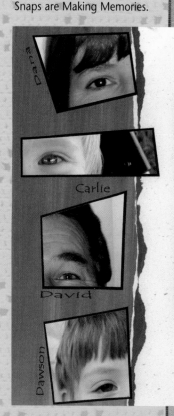

Co-Sleep
by Kristin Baxter

"Co-sleep" —many parents can relate to this concept, when a child sleeps with his parents, rather than in his own bed. Kristin's journaling details the way this practice came to be in her family and the pro's and con's, emphasizing the closeness she feels with her son. This time in their son's life will someday pass, but here it is preserved, complete with visual images recorded fresh at the time.

SUPPLIES: Paper is Anna Griffin. Cardstock is Bazzill Basics. Font is Blueprint.

SUPPLIES: Paper is Li'l Davis Designs. Cardstock is Bazzill Basics. Font is Arial. Rub-on alphabet is Making Memories. Stickers are Li'l Davis Designs and Pebbles Real Life (alphabet stickers). Stamps are Making Memories. Ink is Staz On. Labels are Dymo Label Buddy. Hinge, photo corner, ribbon, cardstock tag and acrylic paint are Making Memories. Brad is All My Memories. Ric Rac is The Trim Shop.

My Very Special, Very Lovely Daughter
by Shelly Umbanhowar

Shelly based this layout on a piece called "Welcome to Holland" by Emily Perl Kingsley. This layout shows real promise for a small theme album. You could create layouts that feature different aspects of "Holland" you've encountered in your relationship with your child(ren). What has surprised you about being a parent? What is your day like with your child? What do you do together? What does your child do that makes her your "Very Special, Very Lovely Daughter"? Listing out these specifics will just make it all that more meaningful.

June 2003 – Jan 2004

When all of our nieces and nephews live so far apart, from North Carolina, to Minnesota and California, it's rare for us to see them all within such a short time span. I had hoped to be able to say that we saw them all in 2003, but we weren't able to see Thomas and Kayleen in that year. We were fortunate, however, to be able to see them the first day of 2004 at Karen & Aarons'. So, here they are, all of our nieces and nephews...our kids first cousins, arranged in attempted age order. I was bummed to find when I put together this book that I hadn't taken a picture of Brent. He's very elusive is Brent, so I copied his school picture. All of the other photos are mine.

Jordanna June 2003

Derek

Logan, Allan, Evan, Greta, Alex, Jordanna and Shane

Cousins Tag Book
by Sharyn Tormanen

"This tag book idea was inspired by Annie Wheatcraft at ScrapsAhoy.com," explains Sharyn. "I enjoyed a tag book she made about her daughter and couldn't wait to try a tag book of my own! All of our nieces and nephews live so far apart, from North Carolina, to Minnesota and California, it's rare for us to see them all within such a short time span." This tag book allows her to enjoy them all in one place at one time!

SUPPLIES: Cardstock is Bazzill Basics. Font is Papyrus. Stickers are Creative Imaginations. Letter stamps are Making Memories. Paint is Delta.

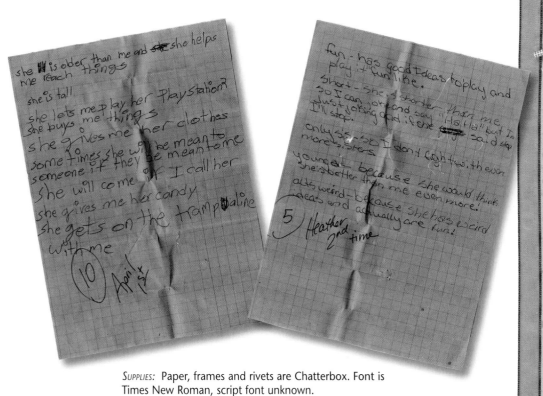

SUPPLIES: Paper, frames and rivets are Chatterbox. Font is Times New Roman, script font unknown.

Sisters
by Dana Swords

Dana asked her stepdaughters to write a list of what they like best about each other. "My stepdaughters have totally different personalities (like most sisters!)," explained Dana. "It took the older one two tries to come up with a list of 'nice' things about her sister. The younger one could have written a book of things she admires about her sister." Check out Dana's cute sewn pockets that hold each girl's handwritten lists. What a useful exercise to remind your kids that they like each other or to do with your own siblings.

Heather and April - July, 2003

Heather's list   April's list

Sisters: *noun* a female who has one or both parents in common with another.

Sisters

Two girls caught in a very unique lifelong relationship.

One would give you the shirt off of her back without hesitating and one would yank the shirt off of your back without hesitating.

During a weekend visitation that was loaded with bickering and fighting David had the girls write down some 'nice' things about each other.

What I like about my sister...

April's list

She is older than me and she helps me reach things.

She is tall.

She will come if I call her.

She lets me play her Playstation

She buys me things.

She gives me her clothes.

Sometimes she will be mean to someone if they be mean to me.

She gives me her candy.

She gets on the trampoline with me.

Heather's list

Fun- has good ideas to play and play it fun like.

Short – she is shorter than me so I can joke and say "Ha Ha" but I'm just joking and if she said stop I'll stop.

Only sis- so I don't fight with even more sisters.

Younger – because she would think she is better than me even more!

Acts weird – because she has weird ideas and actually are fun!

Lists made 20002

Two's company, three's a group! Group "Us" albums look at friends, classmates, co-workers, club members and more. The interplay between group members creates many storytelling opportunities.

SUPPLIES *(ABOVE):* Layouts by Leslie McFarlane. Paper, snaps and diecuts are Chatterbox. Font is RagTag by 2 Peas in a Bucket. Frame stamp is Stampers Anonymous. Alphabet stamps are Personal Stamp Exchange, Close To My Heart and EK Success. Ink is Versamark. Embossing powder is Judikins. Silver corners are Jest Charming.

SUPPLIES *(RIGHT):* Layouts by Elyse Fenerty. Tags are Avery. Eyelets are ilets. Fiber is Fibers By The Yard. Wire is Artistic Wire. Ink is Staz-On. Quotes are My Mind's Eye.

The Book of OSS
by The One Scrappy Site Creative Team

The members of the design team for One Scrappy Site got together and each created a page for this gift book, presented to me and my husband David as a surprise. Not only was this a meaningful gift for us, it also helps us present the talents of our design team members to manufacturers at trade shows. In essence, it has become a powerful scrap-brochure that benefits the Web site and our talented team.

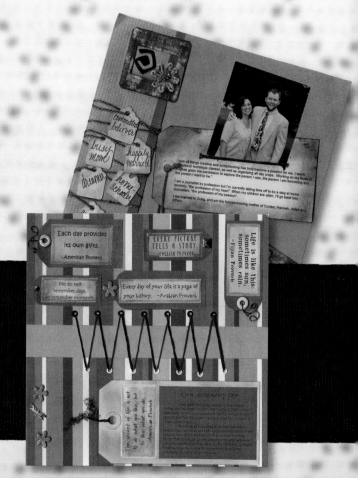

Teammates

...All of us are we . . .and everyone else is they.
                    —Kipling

If you want a thing well done, get a couple of old broads to do it.
                    —Bette Davis

We don't accomplish anything in this world alone ... and whatever happens is the result of the whole tapestry of one's life and all the weavings of individual threads from one to another that creates something.
                    —Sandra Day O'Connor

When I first moved to my current home, I decided to seek out a Moms and Tots group, where I could meet other mothers with young children. Being the get-involved kind of person I am, I soon became Membership Chairperson. I put together a membership packet to mail out that would describe and present our group to prospective members.

Now that I am a scrapbooker, I realize that a small album could also help promote a group. In creating an album about your group, you are basically trying to describe what your group is like, what its best features are, why it's special to you, who the members are, what you do together, and other such information. This could be thought of as a kind of scrapbook "brochure", as well as a celebration of your time together.

In creating a "scrap-brochure" for your group, you could include sections on:

❑ The history or formation of the group
❑ The group's mission, motto or tagline
❑ The group's members (a roster)
❑ Features of group membership
❑ Annual highlights, events and activities
❑ Testimonials from members
❑ Looking forward (the future of the group)

Of course, creating a scrapbook about a group of people doesn't have to be about promoting or marketing the group – you may just want to create layouts about the fun you've had with your friends! Please do so! When you do layouts about a group, you're basically trying to

Charlotte's Web Altered Book
by Christina Foran

Another group you might consider scrapping is the cast of a theatrical production. This altered book project is a work in progress for Christina. She is creating it to preserve her memories of participating in a community theatre play (she was Charlotte!) She is using an actual paperback of Charlotte's Web for the base, so she can mirror the story with lines from the play. Her introduction page features a photo of the entire cast, which she has labeled with individual names. She plans to create pages about individual cast members, and how their personalities added to the success of the production. She also plans to journal about how the play impacted her life, and how her relationships with other cast members made the experience so memorable.

SUPPLIES: Paper is Papers and More. Cardstock is Wassau. Fonts are Curlz, 5th Grader, Dymo Font Inverse and Agency FB. Flax is Scrapworks. Scrapbook Stitches are Making Memories. Inks are Ranger.

Teammates

Chapter 1
Before Breakfast

"WHERE'S Papa going with that ax?" said Fern to her mother as they were setting the table for breakfast. "Out to the hoghouse," replied Mrs. Arable. "Some pigs were born last night."

"I don't see why he needs an ax," continued Fern, who was only eight.

"Well," said her mother, "one of the pigs is a runt. It's very small and weak. MRS. ARABLE (offstage). Well, one of the pigs is a runt. It's very small and weak. (WILBUR looks about in alarm, then points to himself and mouths "me?") So your father has decided to do away with it. (WILBUR runs to a downstage corner in fear.)

FERN (offstage). I've got to stop him.

"Do away with it?" shrieked Fern. "You mean kill it? Just because it's smaller than the others?"

Mrs. Arable put a pitcher of cream on the table.

"Don't yell, Fern!" she said.

(FERN, a young girl, enters hurriedly.)

Fern pushed a chair out of the way and ran outdoors. The grass was wet and the earth smelled of springtime.

FERN. Papa can't kill it just because it's smaller than the others.

One Tuesday night in November, we stood together as a cast for *Charlotte's Web*. Auditions had ended, and the decision makers had cast the parts for *Charlotte's Web*. At our first practice, a read-through, we introduced ourselves with a name, age, and a fact (or fiction) about previous criminal activity. I had attended small Christian schools all my life, and the play presented me with an opportunity to meet new people and build relationship outside my small Christian bubble.

Charlotte's Web

CHARLOTTE'S WEB
A Full-Length Play
for Four to Nine Men, Five to Ten Women,
Flexible Ensemble Group*

CHARACTERS

You need to get up in the morning and say, "Boy, I'm going to—in my own stupid way—save the world today."
—Carol Bellamy

No one can go it alone. Somewhere along the way is the person who gives you that job, who has faith that you can make it. And everyone has something to work with, if only he will look for it.
—Grace Gil Olivarez

To accomplish great things, we must not only act, but also dream; not only plan, but also believe.
—Anatole France

By working together, pooling our resources and building on our strengths, we can accomplish great things.
—Ronald Reagan

The people with whom you work reflect your own attitude. If you are suspicious, unfriendly and condescending, you will find these unlovely traits echoed all about you. But if you are on your best behavior, you will bring out the best in the persons with whom you are going to spend most of your waking hours.
—Beatrice Vincent

Teammates

Sweet Home Indiana
by Jann Fujimoto

"Homecoming is about participating in the Alumni Band, renewing friendships and returning to campus," writes Jann. "It gives me a chance to once again be a part of something steeped in tradition, something that inherently will not change...." Jann describes her memories and what it was like to return to play in the Alumni Band after she had graduated. Her journaling comments on the changes she noticed, as well as what she feels will always stay the same. You can think of groups in which you've participated, and jot down similar memories.

answer the questions, "Who are these people and what do they do together? Why are they together? How do you know they care about each other?"

Why is this theme important?

Being a member of a group is about teamwork. It's about being a part of something bigger than yourself, and working together with other like-minded people to achieve something—even if that goal is something as simple as relaxing and enjoying yourself. It's that "working together" part that makes the relationships between group members so important.

The success of a group depends greatly on the interaction of its members. A Book of Us about a group can describe and highlight those relationships, building on what you've already experienced as a participant. Scrapbooking about groups reveals your interests and how you choose to spend your time. You can also use scrapbooking to emphasize how the relationships between group members add meaning to the experiences within the group.

In your scrapbook...

Use your scrapbooking products and knowledge to create a "scrap-brochure" for your group. Include basic information on the group's history, its members, its activities, group benefits, and membership opportunities.

Supplies: Cardstock and vellum by Paperbilities. Font is Parisian BT. Star eyelets are Making Memories.

Think of small groups that are part of a bigger whole, such as a scout den, a camp cabin, or a local chapter of a national organization. These small groups may change from year to year, so you could do an album highlighting each small group during your membership in the larger group, or you could do one layout with pictures of several individual small groups, and general journaling about what the group is, following the train of thought offered in the prompts below.

Create an album about various groups or clubs in which you participate, combining your interests in one place. Journal about what makes each individual group unique, and how the group members work together to meet the group's purpose.

Are you a member of any online groups, such as websites or mailing lists? Create a layout or album about those experiences; include journaling about the benefits and challenges offered by an online community. How does being online help, and hinder, the group? How does it affect participation? What is everyone able to achieve because of the group?

Create an album about someone else's group membership, such as your son's soccer team, your daughter's scout troop or your husband's gaming buddies. Highlight each person of the group, sharing your insights on what they add to the group. What does the group do when they meet? What

Care Group
by Angie Pedersen; journaling by Gene Samuelson

My dad has been a leader for a week-long church camp for years. The camp "creates a community of support and acceptance isolated from the normal pressures of everyday life," writes Gene. "The whole experience is built around care groups—8 to 10 youths... with an adult and a youth co-leader." This layout describes what he considers the key benefits of care groups and what makes each experience unique and special. Think of your own experiences with small groups—what makes each encounter stand out in your memory?

Supplies: Paper is Scenic Paper Route. Cardstock is Bazzill Basics. Drop-Cap font is Creation. Journaling font is Baker Signet BT. Year labels font is Dymo. Red tag is Prism Papers. Friendship quote is Hot Off the Press. Ink is Ranger Inks.

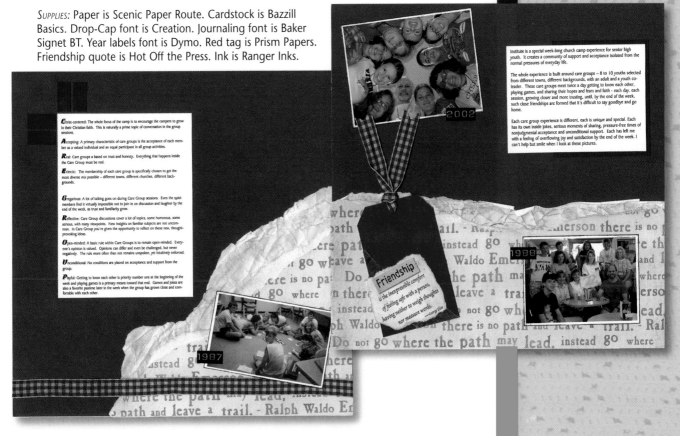

Teammates

It is wonderful to be in on the creation of something, see it used, and then walk away and smile at it.
—Lady Bird Johnson

Men can be stimulated to show off their good qualities to the leader who seems to think they have good qualities.
—John Richelsen

None of us is as smart as all of us.
—Ken Blanchard

are each person's special talents, nicknames, habits, etc? Why does your son, daughter, husband, etc. enjoy participating?

Create layouts on a group of friends that don't have formal meetings or a mission statement. When did they first start hanging out together? What are their favorite activities together? What are each person's strengths within the group? Include specific anecdotes that help highlight the bond of friendship between them.

Relentless Brutality
by Angie Pedersen

Consider scrapping other groups you come in contact with, not just ones in which you participate. This layout documents my husband's computer gaming group. They game over the Internet a couple of nights a week, and every few months they invade

Prompts to trigger journaling

❏ How and why was the group formed?

❏ What is the group's purpose or mission?

❏ What have been some highlights in the group's history? Include other members' input as well or get one highlight from each member.

❏ What events do you have annually?

❏ What does each member like best about the group? What was the most impactful memory

our home for an all-day LAN party. I'm involved because I make the munchies and clear the kids out for the day. I found most of the journaling on the group's website. Think of groups related to your kids or husband—take some pictures of the group in action, journal about how the group was formed and what the group does.

SUPPLIES: Cardstock is Bazzill Basics. Fonts are Doodle and Unreal Tournament. Brads are Boxer Scrapbooks. Ink is Ranger Inks. Transparency is Great White.

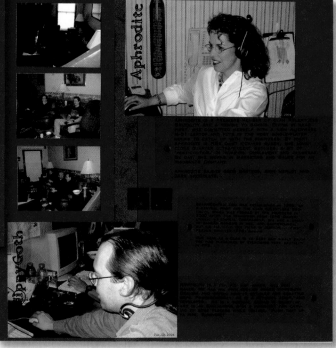

Teammates

Artist Group
by Jill Lazuka

Jill is a member of a group that started three years ago as a YahooGroups.com list. The list has since disbanded, but some members kept in touch. "They became a support to each other, both creatively and emotionally," wrote Jill. This album documents a weekend getaway the group planned to work on various creative projects. Jill's journaling reflects the nurturing spirit of this group: "From sunrise to well beyond sunset, all the creative energy and emotions you can imagine continued to be shared among this group of friends..." she wrote. In working on similar albums, let your journaling illustrate the distinctive character of groups in which you participate.

SUPPLIES: Album paper, tags and envelopes are sarabooks by Hot Off the Press. Inks are Ranger Inks. Embellishments by Making Memories.

Teammates

Do the kinds of things that come from the heart. When you do, you won't be dissatisfied, you won't be envious, you won't be longing for somebody else's things. On the contrary, you'll be overwhelmed with what comes back.
—Morrie Schwartz
(Tuesdays with Morrie by Mitch Albom)

Everything nourishes what is strong already.
—Jane Austen

❑ each of you have of your time together?

❑ How has the group helped each member?

❑ How do members of the group encourage each other? List the three most encouraging statements you have received from the group. Or describe times when you saw members encouraging each other.

❑ What private jokes do you have?

❑ What phrases are frequently heard at meetings?

❑ Why should someone else join the group? What makes this group special or unique? Describe the nuances that make this group distinct.

❑ What kinds of things do you do together?

❑ What is your role in the group? List other members' roles as well.

❑ Describe how you feel when you are with the group.

❑ Describe the group's function in your life—what purpose does it serve for you? It would be interesting to include similar responses from other members as well.

❑ Albums or layouts about groups of friends, classes, clubs, cast of a play, etc.

❑ An album could be done by you as narrator for the group, describing each person in the group, distinct features of the group and how/why the group was formed. Focus on the group dynamics aspect of the relationship.

Lusty Ladies of Lee's Summit
by Angie Pedersen

I created this album for a local chapter of the Red Hat Society. Their "Queen Mother" gave me the photos, and I basically scrapped a "brochure" for them. I used content from the national group website (http://www.redhatsociety.com/), and input from the local "Queen Mother". The album highlights the group's background, history, mission members and activities.

Supplies: Paper is ProvoCraft. Font is Wright by ScenoGrafica. Inks are Close to My Heart.

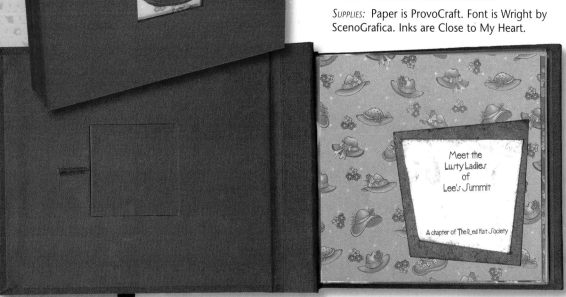

Meet the
Lusty Ladies
of
Lee's Summit

A chapter of The Red Hat Society

Teammates

- You could also compile layouts contributed by each person, describing their relationship to the group, what each person brings to the group and why the group is special or unique.

- What was the latest playful thing you have done with a group of people? How playful are you?

- What organizations and groups does the family belong to? Create a page of logos and symbols of the memberships.

- Do you or does someone you know play a game in a group, such as Bunco, Bridge, Canasta, Yahtzee, etc? Create a layout about how you got started playing with the group, who's in the group, and what you like most about it.

Photos to include

- A photo of group members laughing

- A photo of something you've created together

- Photos of each individual member

- Close-up photos of components of things you do together ("keys" to your get-togethers)

- A photo of group members taken from above

The nice thing about teamwork is that you always have others on your side.

　　　—Margaret Carty

Believe, when you are most unhappy, that there is something for you to do in the world. So long as you can sweeten another's pain, life is not in vain.

　　　—Helen Keller

I am not eccentric. It's just that I am more alive than most people. I am an unpopular electric eel set in a pond of goldfish.

　　　—Dame Edith Sitwell

If you have knowledge, let others light their candles at it.

　　　—Margaret Fuller

Sometimes our light goes out but is blown into flame by another human being. Each of us owes deepest thanks to those who have rekindled this light.

　　　—Albert Schweitzer

When women help women they help themselves.

　　　—Wilhelmina Cole Holladay

Teammates

Supplies: Paper is Chatterbox. Photo corners, brads, paints and flower eyelet are Making Memories. Ribbon is CM Offray and May Arts. Acrylic flowers are KI Memories. Acrylic letters are Doodlebug. Fonts are MA Sexy and CK Handprint.

☐ A photo of everyone sticking their tongue out at the camera (or another silly facial expression)

Memorabilia to include

☐ Printouts or screenshots of e-mails, instant messages or message board threads

☐ Scans of play scripts

☐ Scans of guidebook covers

☐ Scorecards or stats of games played at get-togethers

☐ Scanned samples of projects completed together

☐ Recipes shared in the group

March Moms
by Amy Farnsworth

This layout is about a group of women Amy met on a birth message board online. "We call ourselves "March Moms" because we were all pregnant and due in March," Amy explained. "I have become incredibly close with each one of them over the past two years!" She created a pocket page to hold printouts from the message board. She also made an accordion tag to hold extra pictures.

Who We Are

We are privileged to be members of a group of women—a phenomenal group of women—that first met to study a book called The Attributes of God—The Mind of Christ by Hunt & King. Out of necessity, an acronym was created to help our feeble minds remember the attributes of our Father: peaceful, pure, gentle, entreatable, merciful, fruitful, steadfast and honest. Thus, PPGEMFSH was born. (Let me just insert here that a major component of this group of women is that we like to laugh and believe me, we laugh a lot!

As we have evolved in our commitment to each other and our desire to be servants, showing God's limitless love and mercy, relationships, our mission is to put into practice our desire to be servants, showing God's limitless love and mercy. We look for people that need a touch of God's love for one reason or another and try to express that love through a "treat." We seek to honor those who may be experiencing life's struggles that sometime overwhelm—to show that God is faithful and has wonderful lessons and gifts for them. We sometimes include others who have walked closely with them (in turn, having been faithful to God) so that they, too, may be served. Mother Teresa said "We cannot do great things on this earth. We can only do small things with great love."

— Judy Smith

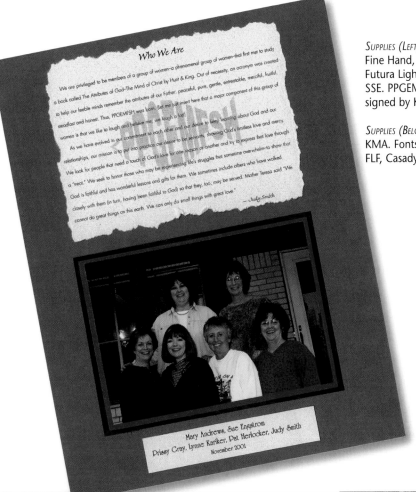

Mary Andrews, Sue Engstrom
Prissy Gray, Lynne Kariker, Pat Herlocker, Judy Smith
November 2001

Supplies (Left): Fonts are Fine Hand, Esselte Letraset, Futura Light and Academia SSE. PPGEMFSH logo designed by Kenny Kariker.

Supplies (Below): Paper is KMA. Fonts are Gazelle FLF, Casady and Greene.

Teammates

Girlfriends Album
by Lynne Kariker

Lynne created an album about a group of friends that started as a spiritual study group, which grew into so much more. She describes how the group formed, their first service projects and how they support one another. She includes photos taken through the years, illustrating the wide variety of things they do together. These layouts are proof of the intimate bond between these women.

Donna Hall, Connie Scherz, Peggy Gay, Julie Leibner, Laura McGee

108

Teammates

SUPPLIES: Tag by Andrea Steed. Paper is Mustard Moon. Diecut flower is QuicKutz. Eyelet is by Creative Imaginations.

SUPPLIES: Tag by Heather Uppencamp. Paper is Making Memories, Daisy D's and Rusty Pickle. Stamps are Hero Arts and PSX. Ribbon charms and metal rimmed tags are Making Memories. Twill is 7Gypsies. Embossed lettering is Dymo Labeler.

Blue Crew Tag Book
by Blue Crew Design Team

Do you belong to any online groups or design teams? Consider having each member of the team contribute a handmade piece to help document the group. This tag book was made by the ScrapJazz.com Blue Crew design team. Each designer made a tag to include in the booklet. Everyone's tag includes their ScrapJazz.com username, their real name, birthday and a favorite quote. "It's a great way to see the different styles and personalities of everyone on the team," explains Scrap-Jazz.com website co-owner and design team member Andrea.

SUPPLIES: Fonts are Verdana and Century Gothic. Ribbon is Offray. Shrink art is Aleene.

SUPPLIES: Tag by Libby Weifen-bach. Paper is Making Memories. Font is Facelift. Alphabet stamps are MaVinci's Reliquary, PSX and Hero Arts. Label is Dymo Label Maker. Inks are Ranger.

SUPPLIES: Tag by Cynthia Coulon. Paper is Rusty Pickle and Paper Adventures. Stamps by Hero Arts. Ink is Postmodern Design. Snaps and safety pin are Making Memories. Button and slide mount are ScrapWorks. Twill by Scrapfindings.com.

SUPPLIES: Tag by Maegan Hall. Paper is Magic Scraps. Font is 2Peas Flea Market. Stamp is PSX. Punch and fiber is EK Success. Fiber is Fibers by the Yard.

SUPPLIES: Tag by Jane Swanson. Paper is Sarah Lugg. Font is Times New Roman. Quote from The Velveteen Rabbit. Lettering is Dymo Label Maker. Charm is Maude and Millie. Fibers and Ribbon are Fibers by the Yard.

SUPPLIES: Tag by Jenny Benge. Paper and square are Magenta. Cardstock is Bazzill Basics. Font is CK. Ink is Nick Bantock. Buttons are Dress It Up. Photo turn is Making Memories.

Teammates

There is no greater calling than to serve your fellow men. There is no greater contribution than to help the weak. There is no greater satisfaction than to have done it well.

—Walter Reuther

Thank you for 💛 being a friend...

Friendship
Journey
Karen Monroe & Amy Saleik
Est. 2000

"A hug is worth a thousand words. A friend is worth more."

Make friends and keep the old, on your silver and gold scrapbook pages. The pages in this chapter honor and describe relationships with specific friends.

traveled

ARE WE there YET?

5¢

INDIANA

down the road...

Where We've Been...
- Coldwater, Michigan   May 2002
- Chicago, Illinois   July, 2002, May, 2003, July 200
- Anaheim, Califor-nia   January 2003
- Las Vegas, Nevada   September, 2003
- Dallas, Texas   February, 2004

SUPPLIES: Album and paper are K&Co. Cardstock is Bazzill Basics. Fonts is 2Peas Magic Forest. Embellishments are Making memories. Ribbons are Making Memories and Me & My Big Ideas. Ink is Ranger.

Funny (and not so funny!) Moments...
- *Karen winning lots of money in the slots in *Vegas (*Amy was her good-luck charm!)
- *Amy pumping in the car on the way to Oprah (you should have seen *Karen's face)!!
- Laughing so hard (!loud!) in our room in Chicago that mgmt. called & ordered us to quiet down! (*We just moved to another room instead!)
- *Amy waddling around #1 in *Anaheim four weeks before she gave birth!

Laughter

Friendship Journey
by Amy Saleik

This album is a great example of how busy life is in the scrapbooking industry! The entire friendship album is set to the song, "Thank You for Being a Friend" By Carole King. Amy also included references about the many memories made during travels to trade shows, and working at Luv2Scrapbook in Ft. Wayne, IN, not to mention more personal details related to memories within their personal friendship.

and back again...

Thank you for being a friend...

Came but for friendship, and took away love.
—Thomas Moore

To the world you may be one person, but to one person you may be the world.
—Bill Wilson

How beautiful it is to do nothing...and then rest afterwards.
—Spanish proverb

That is the best—to laugh with someone because you both think the same things are funny.
—Gloria Vanderbilt

When I think of friendship, so many faces come to mind—friends from high school, friends from college, my husband, my kids, my scrapping friends, my online friends....

So many people have enriched my life by offering me the gift of their friendship. They offer me the gift of listening, the gift of laughter, the gift of companionship and so much more. The times I have laughed the hardest have been with my friends. The times my heart has hurt the most has been shared with my friends. The times I wanted to shake my fist at the world, my friends have offered encouragement and comfort. And they do that each in their own unique way.

When I want to vent, I know I can go to my friend Sarah. When I want to enjoy some chocolate ice cream, I know I can go to my daughter Joanne. When I want to reminisce about old times, I can go to my friend Shannon.

Scrapbooking those essential unique things about your friendships can help honor the place they hold in your life. The key to scrapbooking about friendships is to pinpoint those essential things. What makes you friends? How have you cemented that bond of friendship? What do you do to strengthen that bond and celebrate it? What makes this relationship different from others in your life?

Include journaling about how you relate to each other, what you talk about, what you do together, what you laugh about, how you've encouraged and comforted each other, and what you hope to enjoy together in the future.

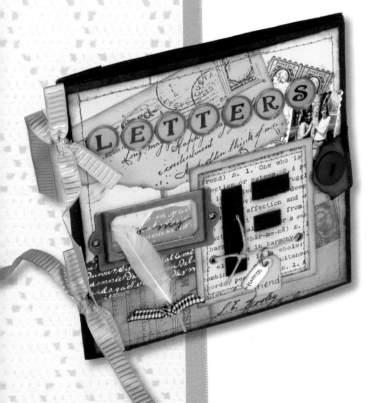

Letters to My Best Friend
by Melyssa Connolly

Consider using letters or e-mails as the basis for an album. In this example, Melyssa decided to write letters because it gave her the date, the address and features her handwriting. "That's something my friend can treasure forever in the world of e-mails and phone calls," comments Melyssa. She handmade this accordion album, using a hook latch to hold it closed. "It represents my friend and I simply because the two pieces are completely different from each other, yet it wouldn't work otherwise alone."

SUPPLIES: Album was made by Melyssa—she stitched together the album using cardstock. Paper is Karen Foster and Rusty Pickle. Cardstock is Bazzill Basics. Stamps are PSX, Stampin' Up and Close To My Heart. Ink is Close To My Heart. Letter stickers are American Crafts. Bookplate is Anna Griffin. Ribbons are Making Memories.

Laughter is nothing but a sudden glory rising from within.
—Thomas Hobbes

I've got so many people who have been involved with me in close, intimate ways. And love is how you stay alive, even after you are gone.
—Morrie Schwartz (Tuesdays with Morrie by Mitch Albom)

Friendship is one of the sweetest joys of life.
—Charles H. Spurgeon

This is my beloved and this is my friend.
—Song of Solomon

"Stay" is a charming word in a friend's vocabulary.
—Louisa May Alcott

Animals are such agreeable friends, they ask no questions, they pass no criticisms.
—George Eliot

Fabric of My Soul
by Ginger Rohlfs

Consider scrapbooking about mentoring relationships that have influenced you. Ginger created this layout about her mother and her best friend. "I've watched the two of them through the years and how they've leaned on each other," explains Ginger. Her journaling reads, "It's amazing to watch the two of you. You've both lived different lives, but somehow you've found each other to lean on. I can only hope to find a friend in my lifetime that is as true as the two of you are to each other." Think about those relationships you've observed that have helped you realize what you want for yourself.

SUPPLIES: Paper is KI Memories. Paint is Delta. Ribbon is Offray. Floss is DMC.

Sometimes the friends we remember aren't current ones. When I think of friendship, I also think of those friends I don't see very often or even at all. I think of what I miss about the times we spent together. I remember when we used to be inseparable, and when we could finish each other's sentences.

Creating scrapbook layouts about friendships from your past gives you a chance to celebrate those relationships that still hold a place in your heart, if not in your current schedule. This can offer a powerful example for children in your life, demonstrating that while relationships often change, and sometimes fade, they still deserve credit for adding something to your life.

Why is this theme important?

Outside of family, friendships are arguably the most influential relationships in your life. You could even say that friends are the family you choose.

Friendships often form the basis for romantic relationships, as well as guiding relationships with the rest of society. By scrapbooking about these relationships, you can illustrate why your friends are so important to you. You can demonstrate what it takes to be a friend and the joys and benefits of having friends.

Someone in your life may wonder how to maintain lifelong friendships or keep long-distance friendships alive. Someone in your life may wonder how a friend could be closer

to you than a sister. Your scrapbooks can provide those answers.

In your scrapbook…

Do layouts for friendships where distance is not a factor. Kristin Taylor's "Friends Near and Far" layout gives a neat idea for using a map to show where friends live. Include correspondence between you and journal about what you do to keep your friendship alive.

Compile a friendship album like Breanne Crawford's on page 122—one album, with layouts about individual friends and how each relationship enriches your life. Describe what is unique about each relationship and how you interact with each other. You could also use Linda de Los Reyes' idea on page 123 to create mini-booklets about each girlfriend, and include them on one layout.

Create an album that pairs your favorite quotes or poems about friendship with pictures of you and your friend. You could also use quotes from movies you've watched together. Or follow Amy Saleik's example on pages 110 and 111 and use song lyrics for the basis for an album. Place one line from the song on each layout and include appropriate pictures.

Friendships aren't just with people! Create layouts about friendships between people and pets. Describe their signs of affection, devotion and loyalty. What does each seem to draw from the other?

Friends Near & Far
by Kristin Taylor

Throughout her pregnancy and first year of parenthood, Kristin enjoyed a support system of cyber-friends. To celebrate their babies' first birthdays, the group of friends decided to send out postcards with images of their homes. "I wanted a way to record all of the locations of the people we've kept in touch with—and a way to store the cards," reports Kristin. "When I found this map paper, I knew it was perfect." Kristin suggests using this idea for scrapbooking Christmas cards from far-spread family, college or high school friends from a class reunion, family reunion photos, or any gathering of people from around the world or country.

SUPPLIES: Stickers are Rebecca Sower. Stamps are Making Memories. Ink is Excelsior Black. Fonts are Atlantic Inline and Ashley. Floss is DMC.

Friends are those rare people who ask how we are and then wait to hear the answer.
—Ed Cunningham

It is one of the blessings of old friends that you can afford to be stupid with them.
—Ralph Waldo Emerson

The best kind of friend is the kind you can sit on a porch swing with, never say a word, then walk away feeling like it was the best conversation you ever had.
—Unknown

Create a Book of Laughter, describing jokes enjoyed with friends, as well as anecdotes of specific times when you laughed the hardest. Which friend can you always count on to make you laugh? Which friend has the best sense of humor? Which friend can crack you up with their sarcasm? Which friend needs *your* laughter the most?

Do a layout on the Ultimate Friend. Think of all the elements of the perfect friend—listening, sensitivity, caring, laughter, comfort, persistence, loyalty, etc. Think of your friends who embody each of those elements. List these characteristics on a layout. For example, "The Ultimate Friend would have Karen's listening, Sarah's sense of humor, David's hugs, Sonia's get-off-your-butt-attitude and Shannon's wisdom." You could also describe specific anecdotes displaying these characteristics or why you think this friend is the perfect example of this trait.

Try creating a thought "cluster" about a friend. Brainstorm a list of all the things you relate to your friend. Use the actual diagram as the basis for a layout, or use the ideas as starting points for layout topics.

Friends 21 Years
by Shelly Umbanhowar

All on its own, being friends for 21 years is a remarkable thing. Add to that the fact that these friends later became sisters-in-law, and you've really got something! Shelly's journaling (hidden under the hinged photo) described her thoughts and feelings about welcoming one of her oldest friends into her family, and how grateful she is for that friendship. Shelly provides specific examples of the support her friend has provided for her. "I have gained five wonderful, handsome nephews," she writes, "my children gained an Aunt whom they absolutely love and adore and I have the privilege of having a sister-in-law whom I don't have to get to know. She already knows who I am and what I'm all about."

SUPPLIES: Paper and elastic is 7Gypsies, Design Originals and Rusty Pickle. Cardstock is Bazzill Basics. Stickers are Rebecca Sower and Making Memories. Stamps are Making Memories and Express It. Ink is Staz On. Mini file folder is Provo-Craft. Hinge, ribbon, eyelets, cardstock tags and straight pin are Making Memories.

Prompts to trigger journaling

❑ Decorate a page with your favorite song lyrics.

❑ What is the craziest thing you have done with a friend?

❑ How does the other person inspire you? Motivate you? Kick you in the butt? Describe specific times when your friend has been your cheerleader or drill sergeant.

❑ What has happened in your relationship that would make a funny video?

❑ Write about a time when you did something totally against common sense, like dancing in the rain.

❑ Describe a time when you did something that you later realized was foolish. What friend helped you work through that? How?

❑ What has your best friend talked you into doing? Was it a good or a bad idea?

❑ Which of your friends offers the best "therapy" for bad situations? What is that therapy?

❑ Locate a meaningful written letter and photocopy or scan it for a page in your scrapbook. Find pictures to show the author and the receiver. Share a story via the letter.

❑ What is the messiest or funniest thing you have ever done with a friend?

Thank you for being a friend...

I always felt that the great high privilege, relief, and comfort of friendship was that one had to explain nothing.
—Katherine Mansfield

The truth is friendship is every bit as sacred and eternal as marriage.
—Katherine Mansfield

You get the best out of others when you give the best of yourself.
—Harry Firestone

Remember, we all stumble, every one of us. That's why it's a comfort to go hand in hand.
—Emily Kimbroug

Memories of Us
by Amanda Goodwin

When Amanda and her friend reached their four-year milestone of friendship, Amanda began recalling some random memories and decided to document them on a layout. "There are so many memories we don't want to forget," says Amanda, "so I loved the idea of documenting them all on a page." The list of memories is pure stream-of-consciousness writing. "I figured when we're 80, it will be interesting to remember the style in which we spoke," Amanda chuckles.

SUPPLIES: Paper is KI Memories, Chatterbox and Deluxe Designs. Cardstock is KMA. Font is American Typewriter. Diecut by Deluxe Designs. Typewriter key is 7Gypsies. Stamp is PSX. Punch is Fiskars.

- Describe some "You had to be there" moments or private jokes

- What defining things does each of you bring to the relationship?

- What would your friends say is your true calling? Are they correct? Why or why not? How do they encourage you to fulfill that calling?

- What movies do you enjoy watching together? Consider compiling quotes that you like to repeat to each other.

- In a dream, you're visited by a friend you've not seen for a long time. Describe the conversation that takes place.

- Write a "fan letter" to one of your friends, extolling their many virtues. Be sure to include specific anecdotes that illustrate those virtues.

- Make a list of unusual topics you've discussed during your friendship.

- Describe a time when you needed to talk to someone and your friend was the first person you thought of. How did you know she or he would understand?

- Think of one specific friend and create a list such as "Our Secrets to Happiness" or "Our Keys to Happiness."

SUPPLIES: Paper is KI Memories and American Crafts. Stickers are Wordsworth and Mrs. Grossman's.

A Boy & His Dog & These Eyes
by April Mensik

Not all friends are human. In these layouts, April demonstrates the friends we find in pets. Her journaling provides examples of how this dog protects, cares for and loves both

April and her husband. Sounds like friendship to me! The "Boy" layout was based on a OneScrappySite.com journaling challenge about making a quick little list of what a specific picture says to you. The "These Eyes" layout is based on a challenge about capturing the eyes of family members on film—and Sam is definitely a member of the Mensik family!

Photos to include

- ❏ A picture of you and your friend laughing or hugging
- ❏ A picture of each of you individually
- ❏ A picture of you doing something you enjoy together
- ❏ A picture of your hands clasped (or hands and paws)
- ❏ A close-up shot of your eyes and your friend's eyes (to describe how you "see" each other)
- ❏ A picture of you being silly together

Memorabilia to include

- ❏ Printouts of e-mails
- ❏ Internet images for movies or TV shows you enjoy watching together
- ❏ A map illustrating places you've gone together or how far you live from each other
- ❏ Stick figure drawings or caricatures of each of you
- ❏ Scans of pet collars
- ❏ Scans of pet paws

There are hundreds of languages in the world, but a smile speaks them all.

—Unknown

A friend is a person with whom I may be sincere. Before him, I may think aloud.

—Ralph Waldo Emerson

Girlfriends Then & Now
by Kitty Foster

Kitty's journaling tells the story of how she met and got to know her friend over 15 years ago. Her words also describe "a simple but not angry falling out", followed eventually by a reconciliation. It's valuable to include candid journaling like this on layouts, to provide examples for others of the reality of changing relationships, with the added hope of coming to terms, and making things work.

Supplies: Cardstock is Bazzill Basics. Fonts are 2Peas Burlap. Transparency is 7Gypsies. Spiral clip, rub-on and definition cut-out are Making Memories.

How Bits and Bytes Changed My Life
by Kathy Montgomery

As she gathered these photos together, Kathy was reminded of the many scrapbooking friends she has met online. She took the original color photos and changed them to sepia in Photoshop, then printed the photo on canvas paper. She also reduced the original color photos, made a copy of them and used the packing tape photo transfer technique and attached the photo transfers to the small tags beside each large photo. The small tags open to reveal journaling about the people in the photos and how she met them in person.

Supplies: Paper is Chatterbox and Mustard Moon. Cardstock is Bazzill Basics and Making Memories. Fonts are GF Ordner Normal, Times New Roman and P22 Garamouche. Stickers are Creative Imaginations. Letter stickers are Creative Imaginations, Me & My Big Ideas, EK Success and ProvoCraft. Tag stencil is Deluxe Cuts. Canvas paper is Canson. Transparency is Magic Scraps. Round tag is EK Success. Eyelets are Creative Imaginations. Photo turns are Making Memories. Photo corners are Canson. Pop dots and chalks are EK Success. Ultra Thick Embossing Enamel is Suze Weinberg. Inks are Ranger and 7Gypsies.

·Thank you for being a friend...

Secrets Among Friends
by Lindsay Teague

Lindsay made this page about her best friend for the past six years. "We still love to talk and tell secrets, even though we're all grown up," she says. "I wanted this page to reflect that little girl feeling we get when we're together."

SUPPLIES: Paper is Melissa Frances. Stamp is PSX. Inks are Colorbox and Ranger. Stickers, bookplate, paint, brads and page holders are Making Memories. Twisty Tie by Pebbles. Flower is Jolees. Tag is Scrapworks.

Angie's Note: You can take a number of different ideas from the Secrets layout. Don't be afraid to take fun posed pictures like this one. The results could become real keepsakes. Also, ask yourself what makes a good friend and how your friends fill those requirements. In her hidden journaling, Lindsay writes that her best friend is "the only person in the world that knows all my deepest secrets. I know I can always count on her to keep my secrets locked up tight." Finally, be bold and experiment with different techniques, all on one layout. Here, Lindsay burned the edges of the white flowers to make them match the off-white theme of the page. This was done by holding them with pliers in front of her embossing gun. The gun heated it just perfectly to brown the outside edges of the paper. She also used cheesecloth as a matting component and painted on the fabric flower.

Shock
by Belinda Carroll

Some of our children's best friends are in their imaginations. Belinda created this layout about her daughter's special new friend.

SUPPLIES: Cardstock is Bazzill Basics. Fonts are Eraser Dust and Century Gothic. Metal flower tags and eyelets are Making Memories.

Thank you for being a friend...

Truly great friends are hard to find, difficult to leave and impossible to forget.

College Friends Album
by Breanne Crawford

When Breanne transferred schools at the end of the school year, she wanted an easy way to remember all the good friends she made at her first school. "I literally threw the album together in a few hours, with the main focus being on journaling my feelings while they were still fresh," she says. She includes details specific to each friend, such as where they met, what they did, and laughs they shared. These details will help Breanne remember each friend even more vividly later on.

SUPPLIES: Paper is ProvoCraft and Making Memories. Cardstock is Bazzill Basics. Ribbon is Making Memories. Stickers are Pebbles Real Life, Frances Meyer and Me & My Big Ideas. Rub-ons are Making Memories.

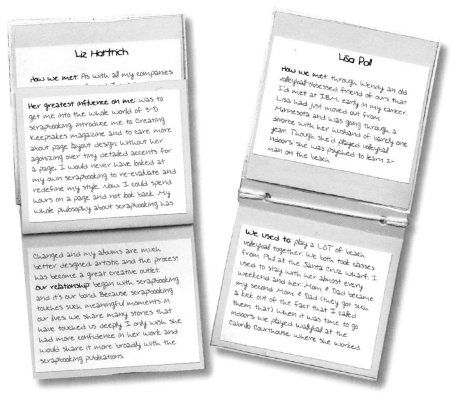

Liz Hartrich

How we met: As with all my companies

Her greatest influence on me: was to get me into the whole world of 3-D scrapbooking, introduce me to Creating Keepsakes magazine and to care more about page layout design. Without her agonizing over tiny detailed accents for a page, I would never have looked at my own scrapbooking to re-evaluate and redefine my style. Now I could spend hours on a page and not look back. My whole philosophy about scrapbooking has

changed and my albums are much better designed, artistic and the process has become a great creative outlet. Our relationship: began with scrapbooking and it's our bond. Because scrapbooking touches such meaningful moments in our lives we share many stories that have touched us deeply. I only wish she had more confidence in her work and would share it more broadly with the scrapbooking publications.

Lisa Poll

How we met: through Wendy an old volleyball-obsessed friend of ours that I'd met at IBM early in my career. Lisa had just moved out from Minnesota and was going through a divorce with her husband of barely one year. Though she'd played volleyball indoors she was psyched to learn 2-man on the beach.

We used to: play a LOT of beach volleyball together. We both took classes from Phil at the Santa Cruz wharf. I used to stay with her almost every weekend and her Mom & Dad became my second Mom & Dad (they got such a kick out of the fact that I called them that) When it was time to go indoors we played wallyball at the Cabrillo Courthouse, where she worked.

Supplies: Paper is Colorbok, PaperFever, The Paper Company and Magenta. Cardstock is Making Memories and ProvoCraft. Fonts are Bathingcap and Jennifer's Handwriting. Diecuts are QuicKutz. Scissors are Fiskars. Stickers are Wordsworth. Buttons are Dress It Up. Eyelets and snaps are Making Memories. Yard is Lyon Brand. Pens and lacquer are Sakura. Fibers are On the Surface. Acrylic jewels are Darice. Template and swivel knife are Coluzzle.

Girlfriends
by Linda De Los Reyes

This layout is proof of the power of female friendships. Underneath each photo mat is a hidden journaling pad that expresses thoughts and memories of each girlfriend. Linda created a "pad" of paper under each photo by cutting identically-sized squares and tying them together with embroidery floss. For each friend, she documented: How We Met, We Used to/We Sometimes/We Like to, What I Appreciate about Her, What I Admire about Her, Her Greatest Influence on Me, and Our Relationship. To add to the design, she mounted clear letter stickers on white cardstock and covered them in Crystal Lacquer for added dimension and shine.

signing!

Beth

Jackie

Kim

Susan

Hannah

Vicki

Andrea

Kim

Beth

Susan

death BY chocolate

pull

Thank you so much for participating in my journal! I've had so much fun in its creation – and it will even be more fun with your special touches! One of the best things about a circle journal is that you get to know the circle of friends so much better. To tell you a little about myself... I'm a wife of 8 years to my 6-foot, 7-inch tall husband David and a mother to two boys, Rylan (6) and Caleb (4). I have been a SAHM for nearly 3 years, and previously worked as the assistant director for the Ball State University Alumni Association. GO CARDS! I "scrapbook" as my side job, teaching classes and designing albums for customers I currently live in Findlay, OH – about 45 minutes directly south of Toledo. This is our 5th move to 5 different cities in 8 years! So hard telling where I'll be once I get this journal back! LOL!

May the circle
of wisdom from
your friends be
unbroken by
keeping the
details in your
scrapbooks.
To make a circle journal,
multiple people contribute their creativity.

SUPPLIES: Mini books are Kolo. Paper is EK Success, Creative Imaginations, Karen Foster and KI Memories. Fonts are CK Higgins Handprint, Letter Home and Plain Jane. Stickers are EK Success and Creative Imaginations. Diecuts are EK Success and KI Memories. Letter rub-ons are Making Memories. Ink is ColorBox. Metal embellishments are 7Gypsies and Making Memories.

Death by Chocolate Circle Journal
by Andrea Deer

Andrea created this yummy album with people from her local store Luv2Scrapbook in Ft. Wayne, IN. Each person contributed what chocolate means to them and a favorite recipe. The sign-in page features Kolo booklets: each participant put her photo on the cover and filled the book with tidbits to introduce themselves. The final assignment: Eat your favorite chocolate and add the wrapper to the last page.

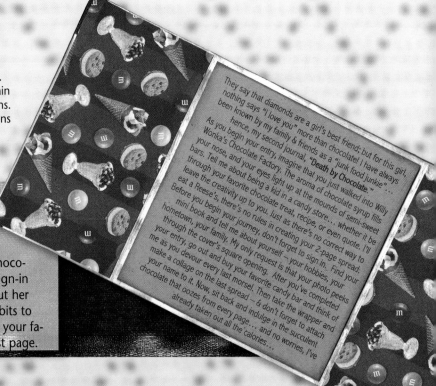

They say that diamonds are a girl's best friend; but for this girl, nothing says "I love you" more than chocolate! I have always been known by my family & friends as a "junk food junkie"... hence, my second journal, "Death by Chocolate."

As you begin your entry, imagine that you just walked into Willy Wonka's Chocolate Factory. The aroma of chocolate syrup fills your nose, and your eyes light up at the mounds of semi-sweet bars. Tell me about being a kid in a candy store... whether it be through your favorite chocolate treat, recipe, or even quote. I'll leave the creativity up to you. Just as there's no correct way to eat a Reese's, there's no rules in creating your 2-page spread.

Before you begin your journey, don't forget to sign in. My only request is that your hobbies, your mini book and tell me about yourself — your hobbies, your hometown, your family. Find your photo peeks through the cover's square opening. After you've completed your entry, go out and buy your favorite candy bar and think of me as you devour every last morsel. Then take the wrapper and make a collage on the last spread — & don't forget to attach your name to it. Now, sit back and indulge in the succulent chocolate that oozes from every page... and no worries, I've already taken out all the calories...

Life loves to be taken by the lapel and told, 'I'm with you kid. Let's go.'
—Maya Angelou

What I look forward to is continued immaturity followed by death.
—Dave Barry

What do we live for, if it is not to make life less difficult for each other?
—George Eliot

When we do the best we can, we never know what miracle is wrought in our life, or in the life of another.
—Helen Keller

Circle journals are not a new thing, though they are one of the current crazes in scrapbooking. In an article on ScrapsAhoy.com, Cathy Lucas suggests that circle journals, or "round robins", actually date back several centuries, "when ladies only quilted, cross-stitched or did needle point for pleasure. She may have lived several miles from her nearest neighbor or friend...I believe that this is why the round robin was started; so she could communicate and share techniques with her family or friends."

Women would design a crafting project, note specific techniques, patterns, and instructions and then they would send the project on to the next person so she could also contribute to the project.

In an article in the April 2003 issue of Creating Keepsakes magazine, Heidi Swapp wrote that "a circle journal is a book that's circulated among friends, each adding his or her own pages....Circle journals are especially alluring because they're springboards for creativity. Anything goes! I can explore new ideas or techniques before they find their way onto my scrapbook pages. I can see other scrapbookers' creations up close, plus it's fun to have lovely, tangible treasures from some of my dearest friends."

What's interesting to me about circle journals is that while they are a shared project on a common theme, contributors also have room to express their creativity and their own take on the topics. The circle journal host offers a theme, but each person is allowed to interpret it in whichever way that works best for her. This means that circle journals are a great opportunity to learn more about each of the participants, on a level not always available in everyday interactions. It's a chance to deepen the relationship among

What's in Your Library?
by Jennifer Wellborn

For this album, Jennifer asked participants to describe their reading habits and preferences. The results reveal not only the participants' interests, but also how books have impacted their lives and helped form their perspectives. Another happy by-product of this project is that now each of them has a list of books they might like to add to their collection.

SUPPLIES: Paper is Chatterbox. Fonts are Space Woozies and Memo. Stickers are Me & My Big Ideas and Debbie Mumm. Tag, page pebbles and ribbon charm are Making Memories. Eyelet, safety pin, butterfly, book and flower charms are Creative Imaginations. Ribbon by Offray. Chalk is Deluxe Designs.

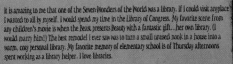

It is amazing to me that one of the Seven Wonders of the World was a library. If I could visit anyplace I wanted to all by myself, I would spend my time in the Library of Congress. My favorite scene from any children's movie is when the Beast presents Beauty with a fantastic gift...her own library. (I would marry him!) The best remodel I ever saw was to turn a small unused nook in a house into a warm, cozy personal library. My favorite memory of elementary school is of Thursday afternoons spent working as a library helper. I love libraries.

All my life, when I have found a book I really liked, I tried to buy it in hardback to add to my own collection. The result is that I am building my own personal library full of books that have impacted my life somehow. Whatever the motivation behind each person, whether it be for personal reading, use in our homeschool, reference materials for talks, or a gift for one of the kids, I have always felt that money invested in purchasing quality books was money well spent.

Tell me about your library. What kind of books do you have? What is your favorite? Who are your favorite authors? What books have you read over and over again? If you aren't a big reader, what have you read that was most memorable to you? What would you add to your library?

Each of you has space to make a 2 page entry. I have included library pockets with tags for you to decorate as you choose. Please be sure to include your PeaName and your real name somewhere on the layout. I am truly looking forward to seeing this journal come home, and adding some of the books you review to my collection.

CHECK OUT HERE

WeLLBORn LiBRARy

DUE DATE / NAME
JAN 0 1 2004 Jennifer Wellborn
AN 1 5 2004
FEB 0 1 2004
FEB 1 5 2004

Faith has been described as beginning with a leap into the unknown...Faith enables you.
—Carolyn Warner

To love what you do and feel that it matters—how could anything be more fun?
—Katherine Graham

Just the knowledge that a good book is awaiting one at the end of a long day makes that day happier.
—Kathleen Norris

Happiness is not a state to arrive at – but a matter of traveling.
—Margaret Lee Runbeck

Dewey Decimal System

The true university these days is a collection of books

Some years ago Mr. Melvil Dewey devised a system of classifying books which is used in many libraries. He chose certain main subjects and numbers, so that all nonfiction books on the same subject would be together on the shelf. He chose these subjects by imagining himself to be a prehistoric or primitive man. He asked himself questions he thought such a man would have asked.

Who am I?

PhiLoSoPhy

Who made me?

reLiGioN & mYtHoloGy

Who is the man in the next cave?

SOcial ScieNce

How can I make that man understand me?

LanGuAge

How can I understand nature and the world about me?

NatuRal ScieNce

How can I use what I know about nature?

AppLieD science

How can I enjoy my leisure time?

fine aRts & rEcReaTioN

How can I give my children a record of man's heroic deeds?

LitEraTuRe

How can I leave a record for men of the future?

BioGraphy HistoRy & geoGraphy

GenEraL woRkS
The numbers up to 100 are used for bibliographies, books about books, and other books which contain information on many subjects such as encyclopedias and other reference books.

KnowleDGe iS PoweR

I love to be in the library. The quiet is peaceful to me. The rows of books draw me in and keep me enthralled for hours. When I was younger, my mom would drop me off at the public library and I would happily spend all day there until she got off work and picked me up. Books were my teachers. My love of reading taught me more than I ever learned in a classroom, and to this day my reading appetite is insatiable.

There was a book collection I loved more than any public library, though my grandmother's. She had a glass faced cabinet that locked with an old skeleton key, and when she would open it to let me pore over her books, the unforgettable aroma of old books would waft out at me. I decided at a young age that someday I would have my own library, full of books I loved. A library I could share with my children and grandchildren.

These are some of the books I have purchased in the last couple of years. My dream is to someday have a room full of books, with a sliding ladder to explore the shelves, and a comfy chair to cozy up with a good book. For now my books are read and shelved throughout my house. My very favorites are on display in their own set of shelves in the living room, where it brings me joy just to glance at them as I pass by, until the next time I can pull them down and peruse their pages.

To add a LiBRARy to a HOUSE is to giVe ThaT HoUse a SOUL

JennScraps

new RELeases

The real power behind whatever success I have now was something I found within myself —something that's in all of us, I think, a little piece of God just waiting to be discovered.

—Tina Turner

Beautiful Now
by Amy Brown

In this journal, Amy invited participants to "admit to the good", and describe how they are "Beautiful Now...right this instant." Amy chose to do her pages list-style. She asked her husband to help her with her list, and with taking the photos. Amy's initial social commentary for this project—the book she chose to alter is a weight loss book from the 1950's! "I went the opposite direction," she comments.

the contributors. While circle journals are a fun way to share techniques and ideas, I encourage you to reflect also on the meaning of the connection and bond between the artists.

The staff at Luv2Scrapbook in Ft. Wayne, IN, agrees. "There are 15 scrapbook consultants at Luv2," explains store owner Karen Moore. "We thought that by doing a round of circle journals, we could each learn a little more about each other. Even after you work together for years, there are things that these topics bring out that you would never know about the person unless you participated in something like this." One of their instructors coordinated the project—each person chose a topic and color

scheme, created an introduction and an instruction page, then the journals were passed around so the others could contribute layouts to the albums. "Now that we have done it, the rest of the staff wishes they had," chuckles Karen.

In your circle journal...

Try some of the topics shared in the Luv2 Circle Journal project:

- ❑ Simply Joys
- ❑ Life's Top 10s
- ❑ Family
- ❑ Let Me Entertain You
- ❑ Those who inspire and influence you

Choose a topic related to the relationship between the participants, such as "Pieces of Us". You could also do albums on "Our

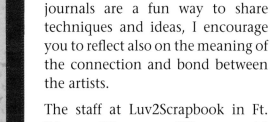

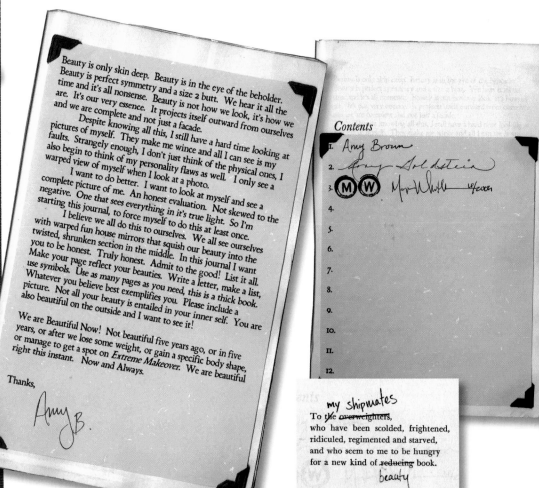

Private Jokes", "Happy Thoughts", "Being a (surname, religion, occupation, etc.)" or "Our Favorite Things".

Choose a specific time period in your relationship and share the memories that stand out the most.

Gather people who have something in common with you, such as mothers of boys or twins, wives of law enforcement officers, military families, sorority sisters, or people from the same hometown. Let that common bond guide the topic for your circle journal. What experiences do you all share as members of this group?

Think of songs that have played a role in your relationship and let music be the theme for a circle journal. Include journaling about why the song is significant, specific anecdotes you have of hearing the music and what the song makes you think of in general. You could print the song lyrics on a transparency or slip them in a pocket. You could also do this same kind of a circle journal about movies you've watched together.

Scrapbookers Michelle Swofford, Kristy Nerness and Tracy Gossard took an interesting approach to their circle journal projects. They each chose topics such as, "My Smartest Decision" and "Five Words to Describe Me" then scrapped them about each other. So, for Michelle's album, Kristy and Tracy both chose

What I wanted to be when I grew up was—in charge.
—Brigadier General Wilma Vaught

Life is what we make it, always has been, always will be.
—Grandma Moses

Where there is great love, there are always miracles.
—Willa Cather

Inspire & Influence
by Karen Monroe

Karen created this album with help from her staff at Luv2Scrapbook. Each contributor scrapped pages about people who have inspired them and influenced their life's path. Participants reported that this was a very thought-provoking exercise, and that they were really pleased with the insightful results. Consider offering provocative topics to challenge participants, as well as a way to get to know them better.

five words that described Michelle; they also scrapped pages on what they considered Michelle's smartest decision. Try thinking of topics for your own circle journal projects and then scrap them about each other!

Prompts for circle journaling

- If you could change one thing about yourself, what would it be?
- What is the meaning of life to you?
- What would you like to be remembered for?
- Open the dictionary and pick a word at random. Write your journal entry about that word. Or pick a specific word and have each person do a page about what that word means to them.
- What makes you laugh?
- What pictures motivate you to keep on trying even if the day has been rough? Make a journal of the motivating pictures in your life.
- Thinking about your life, what experiences have you had that enable you to share understanding with someone also going through a similar thing?
- Using a metaphor, what is your life like? (i.e. "Life is like a box of chocolates.") What leads you to see life that way? Give concrete examples.

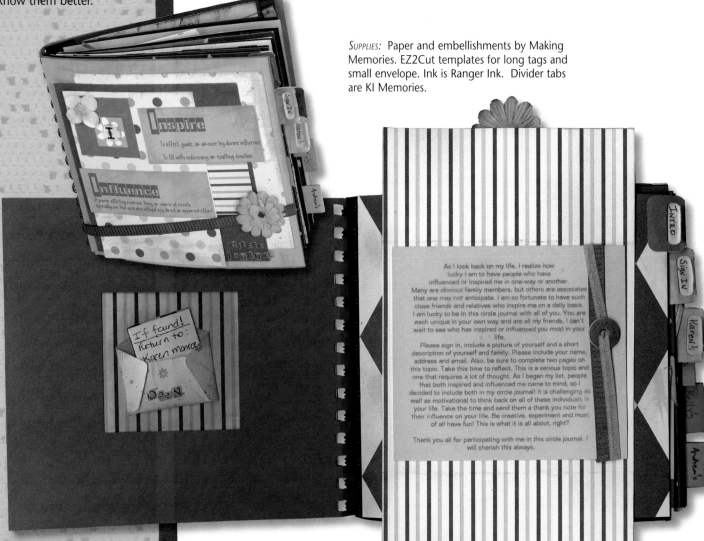

Supplies: Paper and embellishments by Making Memories. EZ2Cut templates for long tags and small envelope. Ink is Ranger Ink. Divider tabs are KI Memories.

- What inspirational phrase or motto do you use to help you keep going?

- Are you a morning person or a night person? How does this affect your life?

- What "Lessons Learned" would you like to share with others?

- Make a list of "Moments of Supreme Joy"

- When have you experienced a personal transformation? Was it intentional or required by circumstances?

- What have been your experiences with "truth"? What is your inner truth? What is true for you? What truths do you hide from others? What truths do you hide from yourself?

- How do you achieve focus? Are you typically a focused person or are you easily distracted? What are your daily distractions?

- Imagine you had to leave your house within half an hour due to natural catastrophe and could only take what you could fit in the trunk of your car. Other than people and pets, what would you take with you?

- How have you been moved by art? Include descriptions or images of paintings, sculptures and other art that is significant to you.

- What are your favorite ways to relax?

- What would you do if you had an entire day all to yourself?

- Come up with your version of "A Blast from the Past", by Libby Weifenbach, as seen on page 12 of *The Book of Me*. Think of several random memories from your relationship, type them up and print them out on strips of paper and include them in your layout.

- What's your to-do list? Think of things you would like to do together, list them and create a layout. What things are the same on everyone's lists?

It is by love that we double our being; it is by love that we approach God.

—Aimee Martin

Only she who attempts the absurd can achieve the impossible.

—Sharon Schuster

ANGIE'S NOTE: All of the participants in the Inspire & Influence journal used the same Cosmopolitan line from Making Memories. It is amazing to see the different techniques and looks that come from the same colors and papers.

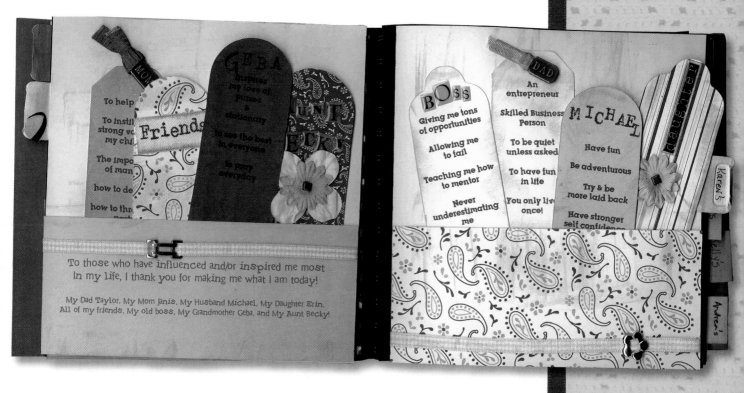

Reflections: Motherhood
by Susan Doyle

Susan worked on this circle journal with contributors from an online swapping group. Each person did layouts on the theme and what it means to her personally. Some ideas for what to include in such a project are personal anecdotes, the names of their children and inspirational quotes. Another angle for this topic might be a humorous approach called "The 'Glamorous' Life of a Mother".

❑ What are your favorite and absolutely necessary "modern conveniences"?

❑ List or describe 3 to 5 "Things that have Surprised You" in your lifetime. You could go deep, as in life lessons, or more simply events like surprise parties.

Photos to include

❑ Close face shots of each participant

❑ Pictures of essential things (to pack in an emergency or your favorite conveniences)

❑ Picture of someone laughing or genuinely smiling (for "Moments of Supreme Joy")

❑ Photos of significant pieces of art

❑ Pictures of your happy thoughts

Memorabilia to include

❑ Lyrics to songs and/or scans of CD covers

❑ A CD of a mix of songs selected by each contributor

❑ Scans of meaningful book covers

❑ Packaging (or scans) for favorite foods you enjoy together

❑ Printouts or logos from appropriate websites

❑ Swatches or scans of fabric from uniforms, costumes or other significant clothes

Supplies: Paper is KI Memories and Sandy Lion. Font is Lucida Handwriting and Antique Type. Silver frames are 7Gypsies. Slide mount, frame, fiber and mesh are KI Memories. Buttons are SEI.

Motherhood page to the right is created by Tracy Wyldman.

Motherhood

I have always wanted to be a "Mother", for as long as I can remember. I wasn't interested in a career as such, my career goal was to find a nice fella, get married, and have kids. So at 25 I met my "fella" and we married, shortly after, my dream was going to be reality, I was pregnant with out first child, it was a girl and we named her Lauren. Then 7 long years later, I was again pregnant, with twins, Alastair & Felicity, what emotions I had for these new babies, I was overwhelmed when Lauren was born, but to see two babies that you have carried and protected for 9 months was just beyond anything I thought I would feel. Proud to have two such beautiful healthy babies. Nervous, am I going to be able to cope. Delight, these two little ones are actually mine. Scared, will I be a good Mom? Pleasure, two pairs of hands to "Huggle" me, two sets of lips to kiss me. Worry, can I give two babies the attention they need? All my fears aside, I am just so proud to be their Mom.

As time goes by, I realize that there is nothing more important to me than being the best Mom I can be to my kids, I want the best for my kids, as every Mother does for her child. I want them to have DREAMS to follow. SECURITY for peace of mind, HAPPINESS to make life worth living. HEALTH for a long and happy life. And to find a partner who will love them as much as I do. I just hope I can nurture their individual qualities they each poses that makes them the person they are today, and will become as an adult. My children have the world at their feet, given the chance they can have the world in their hands.

Lauren
Alastair
Felicity
March 2003
By Tracy Wyldman
A Mother Blessed

Before yOu Go

Boys

The years are speeding by. We blink our eyes, and suddenly the little babies we are cuddling have become toddlers and the toddlers have sprouted into little boys who are speeding off into their teen years. As they grow into manhood, they need to be prepared for what the world has to offer, good and bad. If life is a journey, these little guys are already starting to pack for the adventure. What will they be taking with them?

This journal is to share the lessons that we want our sons to carry with them through life. What kind of men do we want them to be? Which pitfalls do we want them to be aware of so they can try to avoid them? What do we want them to think of themselves? What do you want them to know and understand completely before they head out into the world?

There are two pages reserved for each of you. Please feel free to use any style or product you feel works with the lessons you would like to share. I only ask that the background not remain white. I have included an itinerary for you to sign in with your name. There are tags for each of you to embellish in whatever way appeals to you. I look forward to seeing what values we would like to pack in our boys' bags before we send them out on life's

JouRney

itiNerArY

1 Jennifer Las Vegas, NV "Jenn scraps"	5
2	6
3	7
4	8

CHeCK yOur LugGage

Moms of Boys
by Jennifer Wellborn

Jennifer gathered a group of mothers to create this album. She gave them the assignment of documenting lessons and advice they wanted their children to have before they left home. Once the album is put together, the pages reflect the participants' shared experiences as mothers, reinforcing their connection, even when they don't live near each other.

Supplies: Paper is SEI. Font is Tempus Sans. Stickers are Creative Imaginations. Eyelets, tags and snap tape are Making Memories. Ribbons by Offray. Punches are Family Treasures.

My gUys

These are my funny, handsome boys. They fill my days with laughter, messes, noise, hugs, and kisses. Like every parent, I want them to grow and be the very best they can be at whatever they choose to do. I want to do all I can to prepare them for whatever the future may hold for them. When they leave to head out into the world, it is my hope that they do not make the kind of mistakes that they will pay for the rest of their lives. It isn't possible for me to list all the important things I want them to know before they head out in the world, but I touched on some of the ones that I think are at the top of the list. I love being the mom of little boys, and I look forward to being the mom of fine outstanding men.

1 You are the only person responsible for the choices you make. If you get angry and say or do things you will regret later, you don't get to blame it on what anybody else said or did. Don't make major decisions about your finances or other important matters under extreme stress or duress. Nobody gets through this life without some regrets, so when the time comes that our words or actions hurt another, whether it is intentional or not, make amends right away. Don't waste your energy being angry at somebody who will never know how angry you are. It only hurts you to allow ill feelings to fester. Find a career that love, and always keep your priorities in balance.

2 Stay close to each other. Be each other's best friends. Share your trials and your triumphs. Be close to your families, and bring them together often. Cherish the brotherhood that you have, and teach your sons to do the same. Come home as often as you can.

3 Everyday of your life has been spent knowing that you have two parents who love, nurture, provide, and care for you. I hope you never take that for granted, and raise your children in the same fashion. Keeping your marriage strong should always be a top priority. Marry somebody who will be a friend and a partner, and who shares your core values. Never let anybody tell you that your children do not need you. Don't believe the stereotypes that ridicule men, and don't perpetuate them. Treat the people in your life with respect, and expect the same in return from them.

4 You already have a strong foundation of values and morals. Hold onto them throughout your life. Be honorable and valiant. Work hard to achieve your goals, and show pride in everything you do. Never stop learning and seeking out new opportunities. Always know that we love you, and are here for you at anytime.

SUPPLIES: Album is 7Gypsies. Paper is KI Memories. Font is 2Peas Silly. Eyelets by Creative Imaginations. Brads by Bazzill Basics. Ribbon by Offray.

Little Things
by Margo Rogers

Margo gathered people from ScrapsAhoy.com to contribute to this project. She requested that they do pages on the "little things that make you YOU!" Each person's individual scrapping style and paper choices also help illustrate their unique personality.

margo rogers

I was born on May 7, 1975.
I will be 29 on my next birthday.
I am a Taurus.
My eyes are blue.
I am a mommy to 2 wonderful girls.
I love reality TV.
I have 1 sister.
I love being a SAHM.
My 1st child was born on Sept. 13, 1999.
My 2nd on April 13, 2003.
I love flip-flops
and painted toenails.
Reading is one of my passions.
I also love traveling
and photography.
I love hot, spicy foods.
Chinese is one of my favorites.
My anniversary is February 13.
I am married to a wonderful man.
Family is the main drive in my life.
They make me happy
and give me a reason to live!
I just moved into a new house.
It has a green roof.
Something I have always wanted!

I love to shop.
Target is my favorite store.
Spring is my favorite season.
I love sitting on porch swings.
My hair is as straight as a board.
I have no middle name.
I love fresh flowers,
and I have an obsession with candles.
Fruits and floral scents are my favorites.
There is almost always a candle lit in my house.
Christmas is my favorite holiday.
I love to see it snow
and build snowmen.
The beach is my favorite vacation spot.
We go there at least twice a year.
My favorite beach food is crab legs.
I love soaking in the sun
and getting a tan.
I love to rent movies
and lay on the couch,
and eat icecream.
I have been scrapbooking for over 6 years.
It is my favorite hobby.
I cherish the memories of my family,
and I love preserving each detail.

Margo

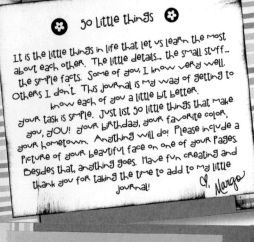

50 Little things

It is the little things in life that let us learn the most about each other. The little details... the small stuff... the simple facts. Some of you, I know very well. Others I don't. This journal is my way of getting to know each of you a little bit better.

Your task is simple. Just list 50 little things that make you, YOU! Your birthday, your favorite color, your hometown. Anything will do! Please include a picture of your beautiful face on one of your pages. Besides that, anything goes. Have fun creating and thank you for taking the time to add to my little journal!

O. Margo

I love the ocean-
-but I haven't seen it in ten years
I dont' have a favorite color-
I love all colors
I read voraciously
especially fantasy novels
I make up recipes, especially for cookies
I love baking cookies, bread, anything baked!
I have four kids
but I will have five in August
I think they are all geniuses and beautiful besides.
I have two boys and two girls.
Their names are Sarah, Joshua, Marilla and Matthew
they are 8, 6, 4, and 2
I will celebrate my tenth wedding anniversary this year
we were married on July 16, 1994
my best friend is my husband (really!)
he is also my favorite singer/songwriter
but really, I love to have quiet with no music when I relax
I hate to do dishes-
I have only had a dishwasher for 2 of my ten years of marriage.
I dont' have one right now.
I have a BA in English Lit.
I still can't spell without spellche...
I graduated (with hon...

Amy B.

50 little things

My Best Decision

I feel your best decision and mine was getting married young. Growing up in the 80s it wasn't really the 'norm' to get married at a young age. You were supposed to start a career, find yourself, and travel first... then get married and have kids.

Fortunately, we decided not to follow the norm and made the decision to get married young and start a family. I think it was a good one for both of us. Ironically, our marriages are outlasting many of our friends who got married later.

Even though being a young parent has had its disadvantages (being pregnant in the bar hopping days, the change in responsibility from taking care of just yourself to a child, etc) I think the pros have outweighed the cons. It is much more fun being able to keep up with Nikki, Jess and Amanda and having more similar interests the we did with our parents. Best of all how can you beat the empty nest syndrome in our early fourties instead of mid-50s! I think our decision to marry and have kids young was an excellent one!

1988   **1991**

Grow old along with me
The best is yet to be.
—john lennon

MY SMARTEST DECISION

Looking back, my smartest decision was applying for a job at the East Battlefield McDonald's when I turned sixteen. It must have been fate, since I lived much closer to the South Campbell store. However, I knew someone who worked at Battlefield, and she encouraged me to apply there. The rest is history, and my history might be very different since I met my husband and most of my close friends working at that McDonald's. So many people who have been important in my life came from that experience, I cannot imagine how different my life might have been if I would have chosen a different career path. Strange how such seemingly small decisions in life can have such a significant impact.

best **Decision**

Caring

Michelle,

Your "best decision" in my mind was always your choice to pursue a career in nursing. I doubt the group of us that worked together at Mcdonalds realized how much we had in common at the time we were flipping those burgers. We all had the urge to go on and further our education, and we all strangely enough ended up in the medical field. Your decision to change your major, and go to Burge opened the door to so many more opportunities than I think you could have possibly imagined it would at the time. It has given you the ability to make a great life for your family and the others that you help everyday. I hope that you realize what a difference this decision made to not only you, but also to your patients.

Congratulations –Tracy

Nurturing

A Nurse is a special person,
an angel in disguise,
with tenderness in every touch
and caring, watchful eyes.
A nurse will sit beside you
to talk away your fear,
lift your spirits, warm your heart,
and wipe away your tears.
A nurse is a professional
who goes the extra mile...

What is a nurse?
A little bit of Heaven
...with a smile.

Nursing **School**

1993

TOP: Layout by Kristy Nerness. Paper by Close To My Heart, Chatterbox and Diecuts With a View. Title font is Gigi. Journaling font is Modern #20. Tags are Junkitz. Brads are Making Memories.

MIDDLE: Layout by Michelle Swofford. Paper is ProvoCraft. Stickers are Rebecca Sower. Font is Times New Roman. Lettering rub-ons are Making Memories.

BOTTOM: Layout by Tracy Gossard. Paper is K&Company. Cardstock is Bazzill Basics. Lettering rub-ons are Making Memories. Brads and eyelets are Making Memories. Ribbon is Offray.

I have a simple philosophy. Fill what's empty. Empty what's full. And scratch what itches.
—Alice Roosevelt Longworth

Nighttime is really the best time to work. All the ideas are there to be yours because everyone else is asleep.
—Catherine O'Hara

Life moves pretty fast. If you don't stop and look around once in a while, you could miss it.
—Ferris Bueller

Be like a very small joyous child living in the ever-present now without a single worry or concern about even the next moment in time.
—Eileen Caddy

My Best Decision
by Michelle Swofford

Michelle chose individual layout topics, then each scrapper completed them about Michelle. So these pages reflect what each person thinks Michelle's best decision has been. You could also do this circle journal where each participant scraps about their own best decision or limit it to a decision within a theme, such as parenting, career or an academic era like college years.

TOP: Layout by Erin Bradley-Hindman. Paper is KI Memories. Font is 2Peas Dreams. Diecut is Leave Memories. Brads are Making Memories. Conchos by Scrapworks. Photo taken by Jennifer Newton.

MIDDLE: Layout by Jeannie Van Wert. Paper is Chatterbox. Font is American Typewriter. Punch is Marvy Uchida. Vellum is Keeping Memories Alive. Eyelet is Doodlebug.

BOTTOM: Layout by Jeannie Van Wert. Paper and cardstock is Chatterbox. Fonts are 2Peas Dreams and Papyrus. Stamp is Hero Arts. Punch is Marvy Uchida. Stickers are Sonnets Flea Market.

The Joy of Being a Woman

by Jeannie Van Wert

For this circle journal, Jeannie wanted participants to explain why they love being women. What's neat about this topic is that, while you will obviously get a wide range of responses, it all ties nicely together within the common experience of being a woman. That creates a bond and reinforces the relationships between participants.

erin

I can pay $200+ to get my hair done and no one looks at me *too* funny.

I get to experience the joy of having a tiny human being live inside of me.

What would my sister do with a brother?

I can hug, kiss, and tell my girlfriends I love them and no one thinks anything of it!

It is perfectly acceptable for a woman to own 100 pairs of shoes and to squeal when she sees the MAC counter.

Jesus was born of a woman, right? Enough said!

Why I Love Being a Woman

The **Joy** Of Being a Woman

Since I was a child, I have sometimes thought that men/boys have it easier in life than women. They do not seem to worry about what others think as much. They do not have as many safety issues to be concerned with. Also, when my friends and I were watching our girls one day at playgroup, we noticed that our boys seemed to get along so well, whereas the girls would sometimes act very dramatic and exclude someone from the group. Further, men do not have to go through the pain of labor, and they do not have to wear make up. They do not have a cycle of physical and psychological ups and downs every month.

Even though I think of these things, nothing would ever make me want to change the fact that I am a woman. The blessings we receive from being a woman far outweigh the trials we must endure. We get to experience the growth of a child inside of us. We are emotional. We love unconditionally. We are nurturing. We have intimate, supportive friendships with other women that male friendships cannot duplicate (and probably don't wish too!) We can see the beauty of things in a most unique way. We have a special creativity. We are very devoted to and passionate about the things we believe in. We know how to have FUN!

This album is dedicated to celebrating the joy of being a woman. What is it that makes you love being a woman? Is it something silly or something serious? Please take two pages of this album to show what it means to you. Please be sure to include a photo of yourself somewhere in your layout. Have fun and CELEBRATE!

For me, the biggest blessing of being a woman is that God trusted three beautiful children to me to carry, deliver, care for and love for all the days of my life. The greatest times of joy for me were first realizing when a child was growing inside of me, the feeling of that first flutter and then the joy of seeing and holding each child for the first time and looking into their eyes. It is such an inexpressible feeling of joy meeting the child that you have loved and felt inside of you for so long.

The **Fun** of it

The *miracle* of it

Pedicures, Cosmetics, the love of shopping, chatting, and shoes, shoes, SHOES, all make

I've Found Peace
by Nicole Bryant

The participants in this project explored the concept of inner peace—how they define it and where they've found it. Each person's layout reflects their own perception of peace, whether it's a spiritual peace, peace found in Nature or being with a specific person. Another angle on this theme might be how you've achieved balance in your life or how setting priorities helps you feel at peace.

SUPPLIES: Album is DMD. Paper and stickers are Sonnets by Sharon Soneff. Fibers are Fiber by the Yard.

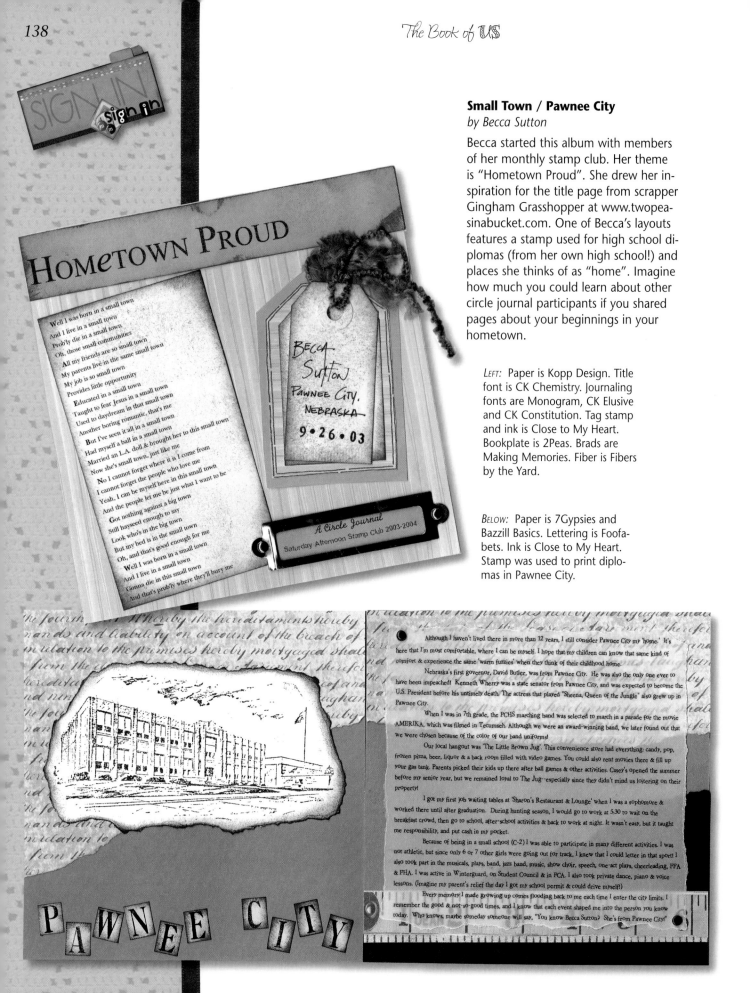

Small Town / Pawnee City
by Becca Sutton

Becca started this album with members of her monthly stamp club. Her theme is "Hometown Proud". She drew her inspiration for the title page from scrapper Gingham Grasshopper at www.twopeasinabucket.com. One of Becca's layouts features a stamp used for high school diplomas (from her own high school!) and places she thinks of as "home". Imagine how much you could learn about other circle journal participants if you shared pages about your beginnings in your hometown.

LEFT: Paper is Kopp Design. Title font is CK Chemistry. Journaling fonts are Monogram, CK Elusive and CK Constitution. Tag stamp and ink is Close to My Heart. Bookplate is 2Peas. Brads are Making Memories. Fiber is Fibers by the Yard.

BELOW: Paper is 7Gypsies and Bazzill Basics. Lettering is Foofabets. Ink is Close to My Heart. Stamp was used to print diplomas in Pawnee City.

HOMETOWN PROUD

Well I was born in a small town
And I live in a small town
Prob'ly die in a small town
Oh, those small communities
All my friends are so small town
My parents live in the same small town
My job is so small town
Provides little opportunity
Educated in a small town
Taught to fear Jesus in a small town
Used to daydream in that small town
Another boring romantic, that's me
But I've seen it all in a small town
Had myself a ball in a small town
Married an L.A. doll & brought her to this small town
Now she's small town, just like me
No I cannot forget where it is I come from
I cannot forget the people who love me
Yeah, I can be myself here in this small town
And the people let me be just what I want to be
Got nothing against a big town
Still hayseed enough to say
Look who's in the big town
But my bed is in the small town
Oh, and that's good enough for me
Well I was born in a small town
And I live in a small town
Gonna die in this small town
And that's prob'ly where they'll bury me

BECCA Sutton PAWNEE CITY, NEBRASKA 9•26•03

A Circle Journal
Saturday Afternoon Stamp Club 2003-2004

PAWNEE CITY

Although I haven't lived there in more than 12 years, I still consider Pawnee City my 'home.' It's here that I'm most comfortable, where I can be myself. I hope that my children can know that same kind of comfort & experience the 'warm fuzzies' when they think of their childhood home.

Nebraska's first governor, David Butler, was from Pawnee City. He was also the only one ever to have been impeached! Kenneth Wherry was a state senator from Pawnee City, and was expected to become the U.S. President before his untimely death. The actress that played "Sheena, Queen of the Jungle" also grew up in Pawnee City.

When I was in 7th grade, the PCHS marching band was selected to march in a parade for the movie AMERIKA, which was filmed in Tecumseh. Although we were an award-winning band, we later found out that we were chosen because of the color of our band uniforms!

Our local hangout was 'The Little Brown Jug'. This convenience store had everything: candy, pop, frozen pizza, beer, liquor & a back room filled with video games. You could also rent movies there & fill up your gas tank. Parents picked their kids up there after ball games & other activities. Casey's opened the summer before my senior year, but we remained loyal to The Jug--especially since they didn't mind us loitering on their property!

I got my first job waiting tables at 'Sharon's Restaurant & Lounge' when I was a sophomore & worked there until after graduation. During hunting season, I would go to work at 5:30 to wait on the breakfast crowd, then go to school, after-school activities & back to work at night. It wasn't easy, but it taught me responsibility, and put cash in my pocket.

Because of being in a small school (C-2) I was able to participate in many different activities. I was not athletic, but since only 6 or 7 other girls were going out for track, I knew that I could letter in that sport! I also took part in the musicals, plays, band, jazz band, music, show choir, speech, one-act plays, cheerleading, FFA & FHA. I was active in Winterguard, on Student Council & in FCA. I also took private dance, piano & voice lessons. (Imagine my parent's relief the day I got my school permit & could drive myself!)

Every memory I made growing up comes flooding back to me each time I enter the city limits. I remember the good & not-so-good times, and I know that each event shaped me into the person you know today. Who knows, maybe someday someone will say, "You know Becca Sutton? She's from Pawnee City!"

TOP: Paper is Bo Bunny Press. Fonts are CK Constitution and Downtown. Ink is Close to My Heart.

BOTTOM: Paper is 7Gypsies. Vellum and cardstock is Bazzill Basics. Font is CK Constitution. Brads and rub-ons are Making Memories.

When I was in college, I only took one 8 a.m. class. It was a speech class, taught by a fellow Pawnee City H.S. graduate, Kevin Heineman. On the first day of class, we had to go around the room & introduce ourselves, telling our year, our major, & our hometown. Kevin started by saying, "My name is Kevin Heineman, and I'm the Director of Forensics here at Hastings College. And I'm from Pawnee City—great people come from Pawnee City!" As we continued with introductions, my friend & high school classmate said, "I'm Eric Eichenberger, a freshman music & theatre major, from Pawnee City." Kevin again said, "Great people come from Pawnee City!" Finally, it was my turn, and I said, "My name is Becca Smith & I'm a freshman vocal music major from Pawnee City." This time the entire class said it together, "GREAT PEOPLE COME FROM PAWNEE CITY!"

Being from a small town, you find that you know lots about other people's business. Even more infuriating, they know yours. Gossip spreads like wild fire, burning its way through town. Everyone knows you're pregnant even before you announce it, because somehow it's been leaked through the clinic. They know when you get a speeding ticket, because it's in the 'Courthouse News' section of the weekly paper. They know when you've gotten in trouble at school, even before you can get home to explain the situation to your parents.

But life in a small town isn't all bad—people know when you're going through a tough time & need community support. Only people from a small town would know to bring food to your family after a loved one passes away or when you're struggling through an illness. You know that if you have car trouble, you can hitch a ride to the service station. Or, if you're busy at work, you can call the filling station, and they'll come pick up your car, gas it up, check all fluids & rotate your tires before bringing it back to you. And no worries if you've left your checkbook at home—you can 'charge it' and pay them the next time.

I'm very proud of where I come from: Pawnee City raised me, educated me & helped me grow into the woman I am today. My niece & nephews go to school in the same classrooms I did, play on the same swings, and even have some of the same teachers my brothers & I had.

I'd like to know about your hometown, where you were raised. Tell me about your favorite places around town-maybe where you & your friends hung out after Friday night football games; where you landed your first job; the home you grew up in or the place where you got your first kiss. Did you have a movie theater? A bowling alley? A convenience store? What do you remember most about summer or fall or winter?

I want to know what you see when you go back home. Does the swimming pool look exactly the same, and do you expect them to sell the same kinds of candy that they did when you were a kid? Is the same woman running the public library? And is it called 'Carnegie Library' in your town, too? Maybe it's the courthouse, the post office, the favorite family restaurant that you think of when remembering home.

Here's your task: Tell me about your hometown. The sights, the sounds, the little known facts. I ask that you do a 2-page spread, but in case you're inspired to do more, I've included extra page protectors. For continuity of the album, I do ask that you keep your layouts in even numbers (i.e. 2 pages, 4 pages, etc.) I would appreciate photos, as they help to tell your story, but they're not required. Be sure to find your tag on the sign-in page, & list your name, your hometown & the date you completed your layout. There are no rules for this journal-you may want to try a new technique or perfect an old one-it's totally up to you! You may use any colors or textures-the lumpier, the better! I only want you to have fun going home again.

I'm so very proud of my hometown, the place I was born, raised & got married in. I love to take people to visit, to show them around & to introduce them to family & friends. Because, as we all know, "GREAT PEOPLE COME FROM PAWNEE CITY!"

The High School Building. 7th - 12th grade classrooms are in this building, as well as special education and music. My parents, brothers & I all attended school here, and now Courtney, Austin & Bobby are Pawnee City Indians, too!

The United Methodist Church. I was baptized, confirmed & married in this church, and remain a member today.

The City Limit Sign on the west edge of town. Behind this sign is the Body Shop my dad owned until I was in kindergarten. He sold it to 2 of his employees & they still currently own it.

The Pawnee County Courthouse. Several times a year, volunteers display the flags of veterans of the community. This is where city & county offices are housed & where they offer driver's license testing every other Friday. When I was growing up, my friend Crystal lived on the top floor of the courthouse (her dad was a deputy sheriff) so I spent lots of time there!

This is where my youngest brother & I were born. (The other 2 were born in Lincoln) The community is blessed to have 2 incredible doctors & 2 wonderful PA's call PC home.

The hospital recently had a complete face-lift & expansion, & now includes the clinic & doctors' offices on site.

My gift to you: 10

If it's the thought that counts in every gift, think of the thoughts that you can put into a scrapbook. These albums can be for anniversaries, birthdays, Father's or Mother's Day or going away presents.

Evidence of Home
by Michelle Thompson

Michelle created this book to remind her husband of home. It goes with him everywhere. The accordion book sits open on his desk at work, and also travels in a box with him on any overseas journeys.

Michelle has tucked little love notes or quotes on what a home is for him to find in hidden pockets and flaps if he wishes. All of the frames, pockets and clips are designed to allow the photographs in this journal to be replaced in a few months time. It also contains photos of their pet and of the outside of our house. Even little cut down jpg printouts of their daughter's nursery school artwork gets put into these pockets.

SUPPLIES: Album is K&Company. Paper is 7Gypsies. Stickers are Making Memories. Alphabet stamps are Pixie Press. Home stamp by Cub Scrap. Hardware is 7Gypsies. Wire mesh by Making Memories.

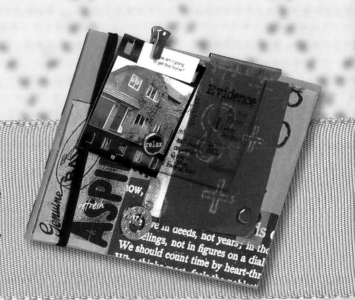

Example is not the main thing in influencing others. It is the only thing.

—Albert Schweitzer

Be presidents of each other's fan clubs.

—Tony Heath

To love one that is great is almost to be great one's self.

—Susanne Curchod Necker

Being grandparents sufficiently removes us from the responsibilities so that we can be friends.

—Allan Frome

Scrapbooks make great gifts. They can fill a variety of purposes—brag books for Grandma to carry in her purse, reminders of home during business trips, thank-you's for time spent together and expressions of love and gratitude. Whatever your purpose for creating a gift book, make it meaningful. You add meaning through your words along with examples of what you're trying to say—combining anecdotes with visual descriptions to help the recipient relive shared memories.

When putting together a gift album for someone close to you, keep the chapter title, "My Gift to You," in mind. A crucial part of being in a relationship is the willingness to share yourself with another person, to make a "gift" of yourself to that person.

Ask yourself, "What is my gift to this person? How do I share myself with this person? What examples do I see of them sharing themselves with me?" By documenting these kinds of examples, you are reinforcing to the other person that you notice him or her in your life. You notice the things they do, the things they say and how they communicate their feelings. Not only do you notice all these things, you appreciate them.

You want this person to know you admire them, appreciate them and are grateful for their participation and influence in your life. Take those gifts given to you, preserve them by putting them into an album and give them back to that person. Look for opportunities to express your feelings with paper, whether with a formal album, a mini-book or even just love notes.

10 Things That Make Us "US"
by Carman Miles

To create this project, Carman attached an accordion style book inside a keepsake box. She and her husband worked on it together as a gift for their daughters. They chose 10 words that describe their marriage, such as *love, commitment, communication, passion, family* and *trust,* then journaled specific instances when those traits came into play. Many children have questions about their parents as a couple. Because Carman and her husband took the time to create this gift, their daughters now have those answers.

SUPPLIES: Paper is ProvoCraft. Cardstock is The Paper Company. Fonts are Bernhard Fashion B and Calligraph 421. Software is Digital Image Pro 9. Inks are Memories and Ranger. Tassels are Foofala. Photo corners are Embellish It. Fibers are Adornments. Frame is The Card Collection. Brads, hinges and eyelets are Making Memories. Keepsake Box is Creating Keepsakes. Kiss quote is by M.E. Bueli.

Love is a flame which burns in heaven, and whose soft reflections radiate to us. Two worlds are opened, two lives given to it. It is by love that we double our being; it is by love that we approach God.
—Aimee Martin

I'm fascinated by a man with a twinkle in his eye.
—Jacqueline Bisset

Life has taught us that love does not consist in gazing at each other, but in looking outward together in the same direction.
—Antoine de Saint-Exupery

Courage is fear that has said its prayers.
—Dorothy Bernard

Courageous risks are life giving, they help you grow, make you brave and better than you think you are.
—Joan Curcio

How sweet it is when the strong are also gentle.
—Lizzie Fudim

It doesn't matter who my father was; it matters who I remember he was.
—Anne Sexton

To love one who loves you, to admire one who admires you, in a word, to be the idol of one's idol, is exceeding the limit of human joy; it is stealing fire from heaven.
—Delphine de Girardin

Nobody has ever measured, not even poets, how much the heart can hold.
—Zelda Fitzgerald

It's a great satisfaction knowing that for a brief point in time you made a difference.
—Irene Natividad

In your scrapbook...

Read the quote in the margin by Delphine de Girardin—"Stealing Fire from Heaven". What a great title for a gift album for someone you love! Be sure to include examples of love and admiration between you.

Create a gift album to thank an influential teacher, counselor, mentor or coach at the end of the year. Either have your child(ren) contribute journaling, or get input from each student in the class. Ask questions like:

❏ What did you like best about your teacher?

❏ What did you learn from your teacher this year?

❏ What makes your teacher better than other teachers?

❏ What's something funny your teacher did this year?

❏ How does your teacher help you?

Create a mini-album to thank someone who has been influential in completing a task or project, such as a theatrical director, sports coach, music teacher, charity drive coordinator, etc. Express your personal thanks, and/or get input from other people who participated. Try brainstorming a list of ways this person was influential in completing the project, or achieving a goal. What about their personality helped see the process through? What makes them an effective leader/mentor? Write these things on strips of paper and scatter them throughout the album, or slip them in library pockets.

Friends Forever Mini Album
by Melissa Unger

Melissa made a point to design her album so that it wasn't just from her point of view. The album covers the history of their friendship from age 8 to their current age of 14. Most of the layouts offer both of their thoughts on a variety of topics: the meaning of friendship, descriptions of each other, and what they'll be doing in 10 years. On the page that lists various activities they've enjoyed to-gether, Melissa also included two interactive mini-albums made with hinges.

Find some "non-traditional" holidays, and use them as gift-giving opportunities. For instance, for "Fortune Cookie Day" (September 13th), you could scrap various "fortunes" you hope come true for a loved one. For "Pay a Compliment Day" (February 6th), you could list out all of the recipient's wonderful attributes. For "Walk on Your Wild Side Day" (April 12th), you could describe various ways for a friend to "live juicy" and seize the day. For "Read Across America Day" (March 2nd), scrap your favorite childhood books and thank your mom for reading them to you. See the Web Resources for links to more non-traditional holidays.

Create a "Book of Our Days" gift album that acts as a perpetual calendar, listing significant days for each month. Describe what each day is, the first time something occurred, and any related anecdotes. You might want to make this album expandable, or leave room so days or stories can be added later. This could be a really useful gift for forgetful husbands! A variation on this could be "Our Book of Firsts", reliving the "first" moments of your relationship. These would make great anniversary gifts.

Make a handmade mini-album from postcards. Seek out postcards from sites or cities you have visited together, then write down specific

There is no greater happiness for a man than approaching a door at the end of a day knowing someone on the other side of that door is waiting for the sound of his footsteps.
—Ronald Reagan

For some moments in life there are no words.
—Willy Wonka

That's the thing the kids don't understand [about marriage]...It's not just a man. It's your house, your kids, your family, your time, everything. Everything in your life is who you marry.
—Anna Quindlen

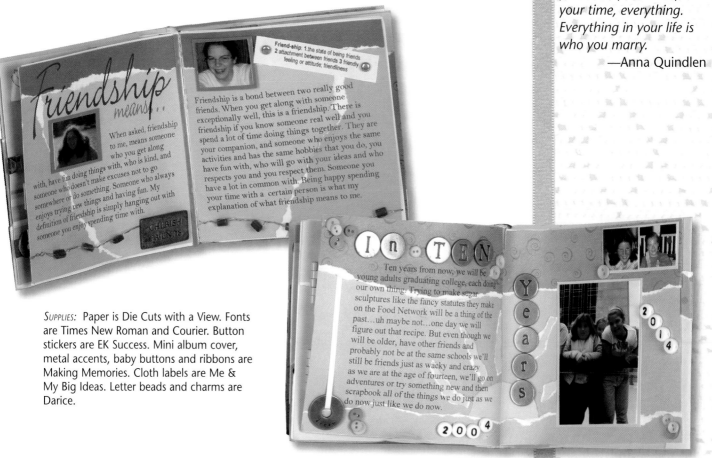

SUPPLIES: Paper is Die Cuts with a View. Fonts are Times New Roman and Courier. Button stickers are EK Success. Mini album cover, metal accents, baby buttons and ribbons are Making Memories. Cloth labels are Me & My Big Ideas. Letter beads and charms are Darice.

Daddy's Day book
by Courtney Walsh

Courtney made this mini album for her husband for Father's Day. "Our kids are little, but it's already so clear how wonderful his relationships are with both of them," she says. Her goal with the album was to highlight some of his best qualities, and include photos of their family. "I discovered for journaling, it worked best not to put words into our daughter's mouth," explains Courtney. "I simply asked her questions about Daddy and wrote down her answers. Then I took some pictures of her that were unposed, where I asked her questions she had to think about and got some great results."

memories on the back of each postcard. Have the postcards spiral-bound at a copy center, or try a book binding technique found on the internet.

Create a mini album of envelopes for someone who travels often. Write encouraging letters to be opened each day of the trip. You could also slip in photos and/or memorabilia from home. This book could be reusable, with new notes inserted for each trip. See the Web Resources link on the last page for directions to make an envelope book.

Prompts to trigger journaling

❑ Why are you grateful for this person?

❑ What do you admire about this person?

❑ What situations/problems/challenges has this person helped you solve?

❑ What have you learned from this person?

❑ How does this person make you a better person? How does he or she nurture or support you?

❑ What does this person add to your life?

❑ What does this person add to the life of others?

❑ Complete this statement (as many times as necessary): I want to thank you for sharing your gift of.... because....

❑ List 10 Things I Like about US

Supplies: Paper is Chatterbox. Fonts are Typewriter and Texas Hero. Stamps and inks are PSX. Metal letters and tiles are Making memories. Flower is Precious Petals. Scrabble tiles are Jolee's Boutique. Ribbon is Offray. Stickers are ProvoCraft and David Walker for Colorbok. Floss is DMC. Gel pen is American Crafts.

- List 10 Things that Make Us "US
- List 10 Things I've Learned from You
- List 10 Things That Have Made US Stronger
- List 10 Reasons You're the Best _____ (dad, husband, mom, grandma, coach, teacher, friend, etc.)
- List 10 Ways You Make Me Happy
- List 10 Happy Thoughts about US
- List 10 Reasons I Believe in You
- When you think of the gift recipient, what words come to mind?
- Use your senses—what sights come to mind when you think of the recipient? What sounds? What scents? What textures? What tastes?
- Describe 5 funny or embarrassing moments related to the gift recipient.
- Describe 5 defining moments in your relationship.
- List "Your 10 Best Ideas"
- Think of 5 things the recipient has told you or said to you that have really stuck with you. Include those in your gift album.
- List 10 things you will never forget about the other person.

Daddy is silly!

or as Sophia would say... "Silly doke!"

"A father is neither an anchor to hold us back, Nor a sail to take us there, but a guiding light Whose love shows the way..."

"THE best thing a father can do for his CHILDREN is to love their mother."

thank you for loving me.

Sophia, WHAT DO YOU LOVE ABOUT DADDY?

"Um... I LOVE His Heart." well put.

- What are your wishes or dreams for this person?
- What things has this person made you realize about life in general or about yourself?
- What moments do you want to capture for this person?
- How has this person fed your spiritual side?
- Complete this statement (as many times as necessary): "You are a success because...." Or

"You have made it because...." Or "You will make it because...."
- Choose 5 of this person's impressive or admirable character traits, and document specific memories or anecdotes related to those traits.
- If this person were to be declared "queen" or "king" of something, what would it be? Why?
- What are 5 highlights from the past year?

Valentine's Day Mini Book

by Rhonda Little

Rhonda made this mini accordion book for a friend who had been facing some personal challenges. "I thought she needed an extra boost of love and appreciation at Valentine's Day," says Rhonda. The mini book is actually from her son, and lists the reasons he would say he loves her if he could speak, written in child-speak: "I love you because: You are pretty and you smell good; You smile a lot; You are a lot of fun; Your toys are awesome and your snacks are good too; You snuggle me and read me books; When we play games and I say "Again!" you always play again; I feel safe and happy with you; I can tell you love me too." The book also lists reasons why Rhonda loves her friend. The construction of the mini book was inspired from the pocket mini book on pages 18 and 19 in Pine Cone Press's The Art of Collage. They had a shabby chic, heritage-looking mini book; Rhonda adapted it into a fresh, clean, bright album.

SUPPLIES: Paper is Close to My Heart. Cardstock is Paper Adventures. Punches are Emaginations and Punch Bunch. Tag template is Deluxe Cuts. Pen is Zig Millennium. Brads are Making Memories. Beads are Little Charmers. Fiber is DMC.

- ❑ What is this person's passion? How does he or she share that with others?
- ❑ What is this person's vision? How does he or she share that with others?
- ❑ How does this person make the world a better place?

Photos to include

- ❑ Photos of you with the gift recipient
- ❑ Photos of the recipient smiling or laughing

- ❑ Photos of the recipient "in action" (teaching, coaching, parenting, etc)
- ❑ Photos of places you've seen or visited together
- ❑ Photos of things that remind you of him or her
- ❑ Photos of awards won

Memorabilia to include

- ❑ Brochures for groups or teams they lead
- ❑ The gift recipient's business card or work ID tag

Gift Album for Mom
by Elizabeth Cuzzacrea

Elizabeth created this mini-album as a gift for her mother. It includes a variety of pictures of Elizabeth with her boyfriend. Look at the fun she had creating it: Inks, Dymo labels, staples, ribbon, letter stickers, sanding, fonts...and now her mom has something to carry in her purse in case of "bragging emergencies." Think of the random pictures you could put to use in a gift like this!

SUPPLIES: Paper is Chatterbox. Cardstock is Bazzill Basics. Date stamp, vellum tag, brad and staples are Making Memories. Sticker letters are Doodlebug, Making Memories and Rebecca Sower. Ribbon by Offray. Lettering is Dymo Labeler. Ink is Stampin' Up.

- ❏ Scans of team jersey's or uniforms
- ❏ Postcards of places you've seen or visited together
- ❏ Scans of newspaper articles about wins, awards, or successes
- ❏ Scan of encouraging comments written by a teacher, parent, coach, or play director
- ❏ "Evidence" of home: Keys, wallpaper or carpet samples, curtain or upholstery swatches, scans of quilts or favorite clothes, etc.

Valentine's Day Mini-Album
by Nicola Clarke

Nicola created this album as a Valentine's Day gift for her husband. Just looking at the photos and reading the keywords she's chosen, the strong, fun relationship between them is obvious. This album would be easy to adapt as a gift for someone other than a spouse —just choose keywords or journaling that describe how love (the central theme of Valentine's Day) plays into your relationship. What evidence do you have that this person is "true" to you? How do you recognize their dedication and devotion to you? Why are you devoted to them?

SUPPLIES: Album is Making Memories. Paper is 7Gypsies. Cardstock is Bazzill Basics. Lettering is K&Co. Stamps are PSX. Stickers are Jolee's, Pebbles Inc., Sharon Sonneff, Shotz by Creative Imaginations and Chatterbox. Charm by 2Peas. Tacks by Chatterbox. Definitions by Rusty Pickle. Brad and metal eyelet letter is Making Memories.

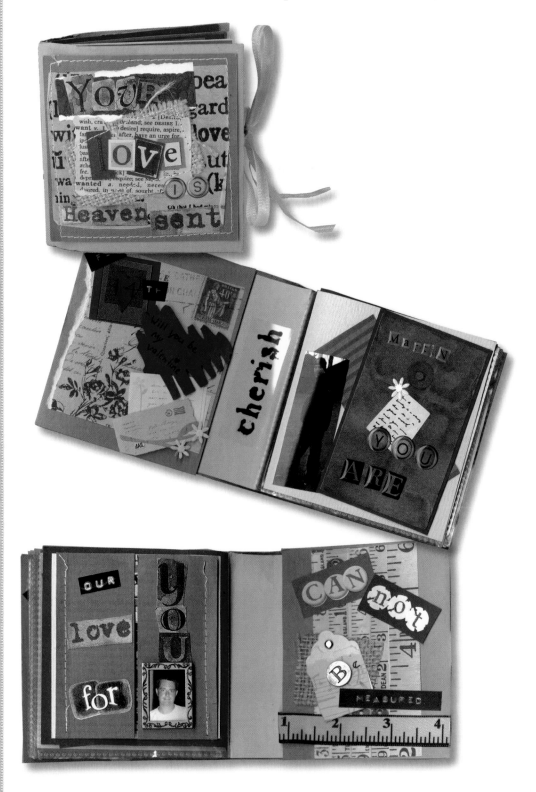

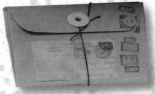

Friendship Mini-Album
by Tiffany Roberts

Tiffany created this album as a gift for her best friend's birthday. It incorporates Chatterbox "Love" labels as topic headers, such as What I Like Most about You and What I'll Always Remember about You, as well as personal journaling on each topic. She used lots of fun fonts, metal embellishments, tearing, and sanding in her layouts. She kept a consistent look throughout by using the same cardstock, pattern paper and ribbon.

SUPPLIES: Paper is Daisy D and ProvoCraft. Page topper is Chatterbox. Font is Arial. Stickers are Bo Bunny. Diecuts are My Minds Eye. Stamp is PSX. Ink is Stampin' Up. Transparency is 3L. Ribbon, metal flowers, brads, metal words and dragonfly plaque are Making Memories.

Book of Us

Index

A

ABC albums 24-25, 29, 34
Accordion books 79-81, 140-43, 148
Altered books 98-99, 128
Anniversary albums 4-6, 18, 20-21, 60-62, 64-65
Awards 64

B

Birthdays 63-64
Board games 50, 105
Book of Me, The 7
Books 36, 45, 47, 126-27, 132
Business cards 87, 89

C

Calendars 13-14, 22-23
CDs 17-18, 120, 132
Celebrations 54-65
Chores 35
Christmas albums 63-64
Circle journals 124-25
Clothes 18
Clubs 54-55
Colors 29

D

Dates 74, 76
Daydreams 31
Definitions 74-75, 130
Dictionaries 29, 31

E

E-mails 89, 106, 112, 119
Engagement albums 22-23

F

Family albums 80-96
Family trees 85
File folders 18, 72
Friendship albums 4-6, 10-11, 24-25, 110-23, 144-45, 151

G

Gifts 74
Gift albums 7, 80-81, 96-97, 140-151

H

Graduation gifts 8-9
Greeting cards 63, 77, 106-07
Groups 96-109

H

Heirlooms 36-37, 89
History 8-23, 102
Holidays 54-57

I

Itineraries 15, 36

J

Jokes 6, 15, 31, 46, 73, 75-76, 104, 116
Journals 15

K

Keepsake boxes 142

L

Letters 18, 32, 36, 50, 90, 112-13, 116, 146
Library pockets 3, 30, 66, 127, 144-45
Lists 38-39, 42-43, 74-75, 95, 116, 131-32, 146-48

M

Maps 36, 50, 87, 115, 119
Military albums 60
Mini albums 10-11, 14, 26-28, 31, 52-53, 68-69, 80-81, 132-141, 144
Mini books 58, 79, 106, 115, 123, 124-25, 142, 148, 150-51
Movies 18, 47, 67, 76, 84, 118-19
Music 17-18, 47, 84, 87

N

Nicknames 46-47
Notes 77, 89, 142
Numbered albums 38-39

P

Perspective 40-53
Pets 118-19

P

Poem albums 38, 115
Postcard albums 145-146
Prayers 31-32

Q

Quiz layouts 64, 73
Quotations 6, 67, 74, 115, 118

R

Recipes 29, 35, 49, 64, 77, 89, 106
Restaurants 18, 77
Romance albums 66-79, 150

S

sarabooks™ 1, 33, 37, 56, 57, 66, 67, 103
Scrap-brochures 97-98, 100
Scriptures 31, 34
Songs 16-17, 110-12, 115-16, 129, 132
Survey pages 51

T

Tag books 8-9, 83, 94, 108-09
Tags 30, 54-55, 66, 80-81, 93, 120, 131-33, 148
Themes 10, 13-14, 24-39, 72-74, 84-86, 110-12, 115-16, 128-30
Time capsules 15
Timelines 18-21, 64
Topics see Themes
Traditions 59, 62

V

Vacation albums 15, 17, 30, 32-33, 44, 49, 64

W

Weddings 22-23, 77

Dessert

**Death by Chocolate
Circle Journal**

Beth's Page

This is one of the pages from the circle journal shown on page 125 of Chapter 9. It was just too yummy not to share!

SWEET STUFF

look inside →

favrite desserts

Carrot Cake

CHEESECAKE

Ice Cream

Apple Pie

Lemon Bars

I'm really grateful that my mom took the time to teach me to cook and bake! When I was a teenager, Mom had a job that often caused her to be gone during the dinner hour, so I was frequently given the task of preparing supper. I really enjoy everything that goes into meal "design," from determining the menu to setting the table, and everything in between! Supper at our house was not complete without dessert. Even now I need a sweet ending to every meal!

Today my sister does most of the meal preparation in our household. (As a tradeoff, I do the dishes!) For some reason, I rarely get the urge to bake these days. Plus, it seems I'm always trying to watch my weight, so some of the yummiest treats are kind of taboo for me, at least on a regular basis. On those days when a splurge is in order, I definitely have some favorite temptations! I guess I'll always have a weakness for that sweet stuff!

154

"Hand Lettering Made Easy" Sample pages

Written by Debra Beagle, this book teaches you easy ways to hand letter and write in calligraphy.

Check out: www.debrabeagle.com or see your local craft store for more information on Hand Lettering Made Easy.

Wedding Day and Topper
by Debra Beagle and Pamela Lange for K&Company

ALPHABET: Stephania #1

PENS: Marvy Memories Calligraphy and Le Pluma; English red and jungle green.

OTHER: Paper and stickers by K&Company. Vellum by Paper Adventures.

Wedding Day Page Topper
by Debra Beagle

ALPHABET: Stephania #1

PENS: Marvy Memories Calligraphy, wisteria.

DESIGNER NOTES: For a step-by-step template to make this page topper, see the 2nd to last page of this book.

Watercolor Pencils

You can easily create the look of water and splashes around a letter or word by lightly coloring in the water and splashes with a blue watercolor pencil. Remember to keep a light touch when coloring using this technique. If you press too hard with your watercolor pencil, you will see the pencil marks even when you add water.

If you wish to achieve a variegated look, add a bit of green watercolor pencil. This will add depth.

Then with the waterbrush, go over the watercolor pencil marks to achieve the watercolor look.

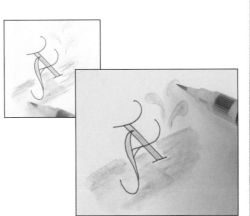

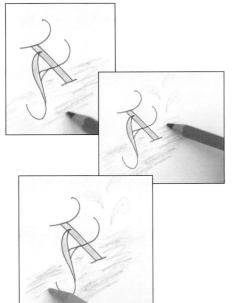

Vacation Fun
by Debra Beagle

ALPHABET: Christy #16

PENS: Marvy Memories LePlume, fine tip, jungle green. Marvy Medallion .03, black.

OTHER SUPPLIES: Paper by Bazzill Basics. Watercolor pencils by Faber-Castell. Tiles by Magic Scraps. Fibers by ProvoCraft. Sun charm by Darice. Adhesive by Glue Dots.

"Growing Up Me" Sample pages

Written by me, Angie Pedersen, this book helps you create more meaningful pages either with or for your children.

Check out: www.scrapyourstories. com or see your local craft store for more information on Growing Up Me.

From Chapter 2: My Family

The Belanger Clan
by Jolene Belanger

Jolene's journaling includes all of the details to describe her family—names, ages and what she likes best (despite the noise level generated by eight kids in one family!). Note that she combined a small picture with a large paper-piecing to give a sense of balance to the layout.

SUPPLIES: Patterned paper is by Mustard Moon; cardstock is by Serendipity. Lettering and flower paper-piecing are both by Jolene.

From Chapter 6: My Character

Hero
by Breanne Crawford

Heroes help us define how we would like to approach decisions and life in general. Breanne created this layout to honor two "ordinary people" she considers heroes. Her journaling describes how these people have influenced her life.

SUPPLIES: Stickers are by Frances Meyer. Font is Times New Roman. Chalk is by Inkadinkado. Definition is from www.dictionary.com.

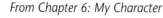

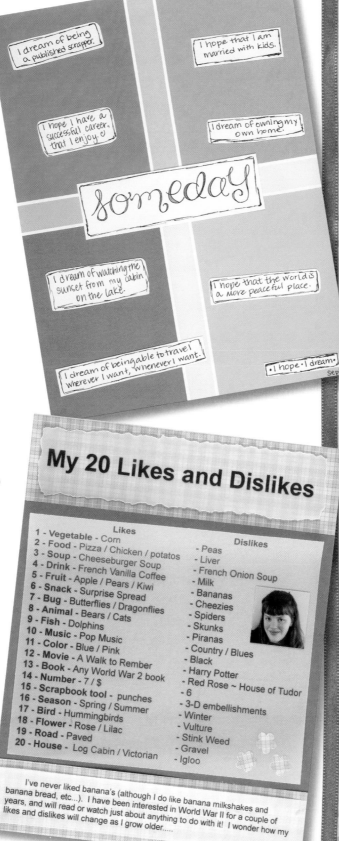

From Chapter 8: My Daydreams

Someday
by Jackie Rice

How many times have you heard your child say, "Someday, I'll…"? The end of that statement seems to change weekly, sometimes daily! Encourage children to jot down those dreams or jot them down yourself.

Jackie made it easy to do a layout featuring dreams—just write them on cardstock and sprinkle them on bright background paper. No need for pictures! Be sure to note the date so that you can keep track of the "dreamer" and the dreams.

SUPPLIES: Patterned paper is by SEI. Font is 2Peas Ribbons (www. twopeasinabucket.com). Hand lettering is by Jackie.

From Chapter 10: All About Me

My 20 Likes & Dislikes
by Rachel Yaceko

What a list of categories! Rachel was 12 when she made this layout. It will be interesting to see how her likes and dislikes change. It would also be interesting to create a page like this about each family member. Have your child conduct the interviews.

SUPPLIES: Patterned paper is by Paper Pizzazz. Vellum is by WorldWin Extraordinary Papers. Title and journaling font is Arial.

"The Book of Me" Sample pages

Written by me, Angie Pedersen, this book helps you get out from behind the camera and create meaningful pages about yourself.

Check out: www.scrapyourstories.com or see your local craft store for more information on The Book of Me.

I Am Strong *by Angie Pedersen*

Again, I had trouble finding a photo of me being "strong," so I searched the Internet for an image that represented strength to me. I found this black and white photo at a professional photographer's site (www.harrington.com). I chose this one because not only is it a beautiful photo, rock is a strong element. I also love how the boulder is lodged "between a rock and a hard place." This is a testimony to the strength and enduring beauty of nature.

SUPPLIES: Photo copyright 1998 Roy Harrington; www.harrington.com. Button is by Create-a-Craft. Journaling font is Desyrel by Dana Rice & Apostrophic Labs.

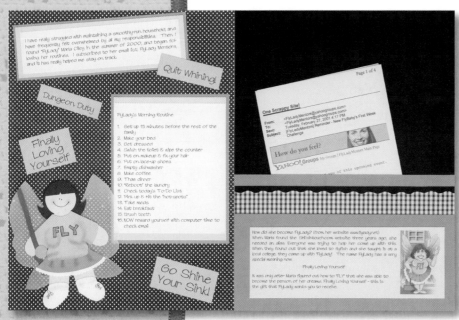

Ode to FlyLady *by Angie Pedersen*

Do you have a mentor or author to thank? This layout honors the struggle I have had with maintaining a smoothly-run household and how FlyLady Marla Cilley helped me through her website, www.flylady.net. I printed out the Morning Routine and FlyLady history from the site along with one of her e-mail reminders that I included in the pocket page on the right.

SUPPLIES: Paper by Paper Patch. Paper doll is Paperkins by EK Success. Font is Joplin by Bright Ideas.

The Journey
by Libby Weifenbach

This was obviously not an easy layout for Libby to do. Weight is such as personal subject. But it was important for her to process these feelings and thoughts to pin down the best and healthiest course of action. On a second page, Libby left a spot for her "after" photo.

SUPPLIES: Title font is LD Fill-In; journaling font is Cricket.

Top 10 Ways to Make My Day
by Angie Pedersen

I compiled this list pretty quickly, just thinking about things that other people did for me that made me happy. Ice cream (#7) is a big thing for me, so I included the cute gift card by Susan Branch as well as a photo of me eating ice cream. I also printed out a complimentary e-mail I received on my website to illustrate #2 on my list. The design of the background paper is really strong so I matted each element on the layout to make it stand out from the background.

SUPPLIES: : Patterned paper is by Colors by Design. Cardstock is by Crafter's Workshop. Diecut is by Susan Branch. Title font is CK Flair, Wedding Alphabets by Creating Keepsakes; journaling font is Joplin by Bright Ideas.

Visit Angie online...

All of the chapters in this book have additional Internet resources. Please see the links on my web-site shown here.

Download free fonts...

While you're there, browse the 100s of free fonts, organized alphabetically. See you online!

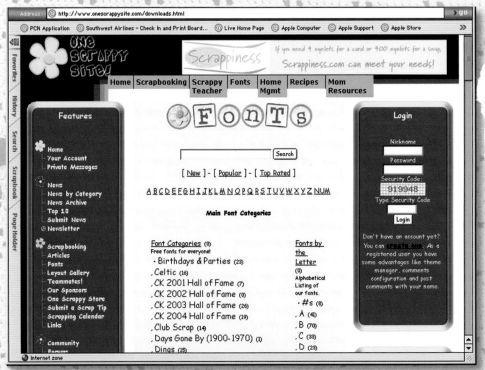